GREAT HOUSES OF SCOTLAND

HUGH MONTGOMERY-MASSINGBERD
CHRISTOPHER SIMON SYKES

ACKNOWLEDGEMENTS

We received wonderfully generous consideration, co-operation, hospitality and practical advice from owners, administrators, experts, friends and kinsfolk during our sojourn in Scotland for this book. We would particularly like to thank the following, all of whom made significant contributions to the book and to our enjoyment in producing it: June Marchioness of Aberdeen, Gillon Aitken, the Duke of Argyll, Tony Ashby, the late Duke of Atholl, Mark Bence-Jones, Matthew Benson, Marcus Binney, the Duke and Duchess of Buccleuch, Charles Burnett, the late Marquess of Bute, Johnny Bute, Jonathan Cardale, Lt-Col Patrick Cardwell Moore, the late Earl Cawdor and the Dowager Countess Cawdor, Niget and Henrietta Cayzer, Tim and Jane Clifford, Philip Cooper, the Earl of Dalkeith, Lady Antonia Dalrymple, Althea Dundas Bekker, Henrietta Dundas Bekker, Lady Elphinstone, Elizabeth Faber, Peter Fairweather, Craig Ferguson, Andrew Fisher, the Knight of Glin, Sir Alistair Grant, Nelly Grant, Robert Gray, the Earl and Countess of Haddington, Christopher Hartley, Sandra Howat, Norman Hudson, James Hunter Blair, Charles Janson, Peter Jarvis, Keith Jones, Nina Kapoor, Katie Kerr, Isobel Kyle, Tony Lawrence at Fuji, David Learmont, Margot Leslie, Michael Leslie, Hamish Leslie Melville, Cynthia Lewis, the Marquess of Linlithgow, Wendy McDonald, John McEwen, Angus and Jane Maclay, Sir Charles Maclean, Bt, Andrew McLean, Gerald and Rosalind Maitland-Carew, the Earl and Countess of Mansfield, Kit Martin, Hannah Mason, Dame Jean Maxwell-Scott, the late Patricia Maxwell-Scott, Catherine Maxwell Stuart, Flora Maxwell Stuart, Geoffrey Mitchell, William Mitchell, James Montgomery, Sir David Montgomery, Bt, Luke Massingberd, Caroline Montgomery-Massingberd, John and Marsali Montgomery-Massingberd, the late Sir Iain Moncreiffe of that Ilk, Bt, Teresa Moore, Lord Neidpath, John Noble, Brian Nodes, Paul Normand, Sir Francis Ogilvy, Bt, Lady Ogilvy, Lord and Lady Palmer, Michael Pare, John Powell, Peter Reekie, Peter Reid, Lt-Cdr A.R. Robinson, John Martin Robinson, the Earl and Countess of Rosebery, Michael Sayer, James Scott, Mary Scott, David Sharland, Peter Sinclair, Karen Stafford, Gavin Stamp, Jackie Stewart, Sir Jamie Stormonth Darling, the Earl and Countess of Strathmore, Lord Strathnaver, the Countess of Sutherland, Sir Tatton Sykes, Bt, the late Rev Henry Thorold, Sarah Troughton, Hugo and Elizabeth Vickers, Ed Victor, Sir Humphry Wakefield, Bt, the Earl and Countess of Wemyss, A.N. Wilson and Alison Wormleighton.

Published in 2005 by Silverdale Books
An imprint of Bookmart Ltd
Registered Number 2372865
Trading as Bookmart Limited
Blaby Road
Wigston
Leicester
LE18 4SE

A catalogue record for this book is available from the British Library.

ISBN 1 84509 107 8

Designed by Andrew Shoolbred

Printed in China
The Hanway Press Ltd

Half title: Mount Stuart, Isle of Bute: detail of a turreted downpipe.
Frontispiece: The sea shore at Dunrobin Castle.

GREAT HOUSES
OF SCOTLAND

CONTENTS

INTRODUCTION

IN THE Sassenach comedian Tony Hancock's celebrated television sketch *The Blood Donor*, the curmudgeon of East Cheam, on ascertaining that the doctor is a Scot, proceeds to address him in the manner of Sir Harry Lauder – with a 'Hoots Mon', allusions to 'bricht moonlicht nichts' and other Caledonian cliché's. 'We're not,' responds Patrick Cargill, as the medic, in his best Sandhurst drawl, '*all* Rob Roys, you know'.

Similarly, most popular illustrated books on the subject of Scottish heritage tend to be tartaned tributes to the hoary traditions of hackneyed picture-postcard castles. Well-worn paths are trodden around bleak fortresses bedecked with sentimental legends. Somehow Scotland's no less splendid set of Great Houses has not received the attention it deserves. Perhaps this personal selection of fine family seats may open a few eyes unfamiliar with this much underrated dimension of Scottish social history?

Naturally, as a glance at the contents page will confirm, many (indeed almost a third) of the 25 houses featured in the book happen to rejoice in the name of 'Castle', that wide-ranging and much misunderstood term. Nor, we trust, does this eclectic collection of places lack for romance or colour – or blood, for that matter. Yet, on the whole, we have chosen to chronicle domestic, as opposed to defensive, building in its grandest forms.

The great houses that follow – in a loose chronological sequence based rather more on the length of tenure enjoyed on the estate by the family concerned than on the predominant architectural style of the present building – reflect the evolution and development of Scottish architecture through the centuries. The early, pre-1500, castles tended, for obvious defensive reasons, to concentrate their accommodation in a massive single tower, adjoined by a walled courtyard. Cawdor is a particularly good example of these 'compound' Scots houses, but such old towers still form the basis of several other structures where they are obscured by subsequent building work, as at Dunrobin.

Indeed the tower long remained the principal 'type' for every scale of domestic building in Scotland. The typical tower-house of the 16th and 17th centuries was 'L'-shaped, with a staircase turret set in the internal angle. Glamis is the most striking specimen of this style, while the delightfully straightforward Traquair departs from the 'angular' arrangement.

The 'Auld Alliance' with France helped introduce Renaissance flourishes to Scotland from the
16th century onwards. Early 17th-century Scottish country houses may have resembled fortified
castles – tall and narrow, with thick walls and small
rooms – though their design was no longer inspired
by considerations of defence alone, but also by
a romantic medievalism. This was the same dream
of chivalry that in the France of François I had
produced the *châteaux* of the Loire.

With the accession of King James VI of Scotland to the English throne in 1603, though,
the Scots nobles began to form part of the British
aristocracy instead of being, as had previously
been the case, the aristocracy of another country,
whether the French-orientated Lowland aristocracy in the reigns of King James V and Mary
Queen of Scots or the old Gaelic-speaking tribal
aristocracy of the Highlands. Now Scots aristocrats who hoped for advancement hurried south
to the Jacobean Court. New ideas and fashions,
emanating from the Low Countries and Italy,
as well as England were picked up.

Later in the 17th century, following the bit-
ter aftermath of the Civil War, came the full
flowering of the Scots Renaissance with such spectacular Baroque palaces as Drumlanrig. The architect
of the lavish late-Stuart remodelling of Thirlestane,
Sir William Bruce, went on to build Scotland's
first purely Classical country houses such as
Kinross and the original Hopetoun.

Notwithstanding the Act of Union with England in 1707, and the upheavals of the Jacobite
Risings of 1715 and 1745, Classical architecture flourished amid the 18th-century Scottish
Enlightenment. William Adam, the leading
Scottish architect of the first half of the century, whose achievements have been unfairly
overshadowed by the brilliance of his son Robert,
designed a remarkably diverse range of country
houses.

PRECEDING PAGE
A shore silhouette of Culzean Castle.

ABOVE
Gateway to the Dutch Garden at Glamis laid out by the
13th Earl of Strathmore in 1893.

RIGHT
The Picture Staircase at Blair Castle. It was created in
1756 and redecorated in the 19th century, when the
plaster and woodwork were grained. The full-length
portrait is of the 1st Marquess of Atholl, painted by
Jacob De Witt (or de Wet) in the late-17th-century
Classical manner as Julius Caesar, with the Battle of
Bothwell Brig proceeding vigorously under his baton.

By way of redressing the balance, Adam senior's prolific output is very generously represented in this selection. Indeed, though not beyond criticism for his tampering with earlier work, William Adam is effectively the star of the show. His hand seems to be everywhere – Hopetoun, Mellerstain, Arniston, the House of Dun, Haddo, Duff, even Inveraray.

If William Adam has been hitherto underrated outside Scotland, so, paradoxically, Robert Adam – who went South and dominated the English architectural scene – has not perhaps received the recognition he deserves in his native land. He was, after all, responsible for the exquisite interiors at Mellerstain and the romantic cliff-top 'castle' of Culzean.

This harking back to the castle style in the late-18th century indicated the Scots' deep-seated yearning for the old traditions. It was soon to be fuelled by the stirring romances of Sir Walter Scott, Laird of Abbotsford, who helped heal the wounds of Culloden by masterminding King George IV's emotional visit to Scotland in 1822. Scott was the precursor of the Baronial Revival, a style which was somewhat over-developed later in the 19th century, principally by David Bryce, who remodelled Blair.

The 'discovery' of the Highlands, which had started with the Romantic Movement and Scott's novels, was furthered by the British aristocracy's love of sport and also by the coming of the railways. With Queen Victoria's purchase of Balmoral in 1848 the Highlands were really in vogue. A surging sea of tartan threatened to engulf Caledonia.

BELOW
The west (garden) front at Hopetoun House.

Later in the 19th century, the amazing High Victorian Gothic of Mount Stuart was rather in a category of its own. The story of the great house in Scotland, though, continues into the 20th century with the no less astonishing Edwardian opulence of Manderston, which adopted the 'Adam' style. Finally, we come full circle at the romantic shooting lodge of Ardkinglas, where Sir Robert Lorimer, the 'Scots Lutyens', sympathetically combined 17th-century vernacular with modern comfort.

It need hardly be said that the original photography laid out here captures the spirit and style of the houses infinitely better than words ever could. Therefore the text is essentially as much about the landed dynasties who created these glorious temples of the arts as about the architecture and decoration.

By their very definition, great houses are the seats of great families. Accordingly, the great families of Scotland figure prominently in the narrative. The Royal House of Stuart is represented by such branches as the Maxwell Stuarts of Traquair and the Crichton-Stuarts, Marquesses of Bute, at Mount Stuart. The illustrious House of Hamilton, in the regrettable absence of the ducal Hamilton Palace (demolished in the 1920s), is represented by the Baillie-Hamiltons, Earls of Haddington, at Mellerstain. The Duke of Buccleuch, at Drumlanrig and Bowhill, flies the flag for Douglas and Scott respectively.

Ensuring that the Lowlands do not hog the limelight, the Clan Campbell fields its Chief, the Duke of Argyll, at Inveraray, and Earl Cawdor at Cawdor. The Murrays are represented by the Dukes of Atholl at Blair and the Earl of Mansfield at Scone.

While retailing the family histories, and not neglecting the anecdotes that form part of aristocratic folklore, an attempt has been made to bring the story right up to date – into the 21st century. Thus it is possible to celebrate the National Trust for Scotland's current rescue mission at Newhailes and its recent restorations of the House of Dun and Culzean. Enterprising new charitable trust schemes have brought new purpose and vigour to such palaces as Thirlestane, Hopetoun and Mount Stuart (magnificently restored by the late Marquess of Bute before his premature death in 1993). An initiative by the National Galleries of Scotland helped find an 'outstation' solution for the 'forgotten' splendours of Duff House. The Galleries' director, Tim Clifford, is one of the residents in Kit Martin's inspiring recent conversion of Tyninghame for multiple occupation – wherein the future of 'problem' great houses may well lie.

Far from the doom-gloom one so often encounters in the private sector of the Heritage world, the Scots joint is jumping in the new Millennium. Everywhere you look there are encouraging signs that the present generation of private owners is taking a much more positive approach to great houses than their often unduly pessimistic, not to say philistine, predecessors. Such dedicated châtelaines as Althea Dundas Bekker (who is restoring the formerly dry-rot-ridden Arniston) and the Countess of Rosebery (who has stylishly rationalized the display of the collections at Dalmeny) communicate enthusiasm for the future. The Duke of Buccleuch has won deserved acclaim as a champion of public-spirited land management and countryside education at Drumlanrig and Bowhill.

Up on Loch Fyne, the Duke of Argyll has rejuvenated Inveraray after a seemingly disastrous fire and John Noble's seafood business has revitalized Ardkinglas. Down on the Tweed strong ales are being brewed once more at Traquair. Happily, for the great houses of Scotland in general, there appears to be plenty of good stuff left in the bottle for future generations to savour.

BLAIR CASTLE

PERTHSHIRE

BLAIR – a palimpsest of Scottish history and architectural taste – illustrates the folly of seeking to impose a rigorous classification between Castles and Great Houses. At first glimpse from the new 'high road' that runs from Perth to Inverness, the elevated prospect shows us a massive white-harled façade, complete with crowstepped gables and bartizans. Cradled by forest-clad mountains and surrounded by romantic rivers at the entrance to the Highland fastnesses of Glen Garry, this, one thinks, must be the ultimate Scotch Baronial pile.

Yet, on closer inspection, the immediate setting of this seat of the Murrays, Dukes of Atholl, exudes the controlled grandeur of aristocratic aestheticism. As we approach the castle we notice the hallmarks of a great house in its parkland element of tamed nature. Although the castellations outside and the armoury-encrusted entrance hall within do indeed turn out to be the work of the 'Baronial' architect David Bryce, dating from 1869, the interior springs a considerable surprise. For underneath the oh-so-Scottish skin is to be found a sumptuous temple of the Georgian arts adorned with Rococo plasterwork by Thomas Clayton (who worked with William Adam at Holyroodhouse in Edinburgh) and marble chimneypieces by Thomas Carter (a favourite craftsman of the Prince Regent). Here, then, is a Highland Castle which, as Mark Girouard has pointed out, became 'a treasure-house of mid-18th century English furniture and decoration.'

Yet it would be wrong to infer that there is something 'fake' about Blair as the tourist buses pull up in front of the Castle Piper blowing away manfully or the Atholl Highlanders (Britain's only surviving 'private army', a ceremonial bodyguard championed by Queen Victoria in an excess of Highland enthusiasm) parading to the strains of the Pipe Band. For – to

PRECEDING PAGES
The majestic Drawing
Room, hung in crimson
damask, with its coved
ceiling rich in plaster-
work by Thomas
Clayton, who also carved
the white marble
chimneypiece. The
picture above is Johann
Zoffany's bucolic
conversation piece of the
3rd Duke of Atholl and
his family. The pier glass
mirrors were made by
George Cole.

LEFT
The Georgian Front
Staircase. The portrait of
*James Moray (younger)
of Abercairny* must have
been painted after the
1745 Jacobite Rising,
when the kilt was
proscribed – which may
explain why the picture
was not signed (it is
thought to be by
Davison).

RIGHT
The Entrance Hall, built
in 1872 for the 7th
Duke of Atholl by David
and John Bryce. The
display of arms includes
rifles, targes, swords,
crossbows and powder-
horns.

borrow a Hollywood witticism about Ernest Hemingway to the effect
that his chest wig disguised a genuinely hairy chest underneath – Blair,
too, boasts authentic battlements behind the phoney turrets.

As befits a castle in such an obviously strategic situation, Blair was first
fortified as far back as the 13th century, when the Royal Celtic line of the
original Earls of Atholl died out. The Earldom passed to the Strathbogie
dynasty, of whom David, the 'Crusader Earl', complained in 1269 to
King Alexander III that, during his absence in England, John Comyn, or
Cumming, of Badenoch had made an incursion into Atholl and begun building a castle at Blair. To this day the main tower of the castle is, by tradition,

known as Cumming's Tower. A wing and a second tower were later to be added, also in the traditional Scottish castle style.

The Earldom of Atholl and Blair itself suffered many vicissitudes brought about by the buffetings of Anglo-Scottish history and the ever-conflicting loyalties demanded by the two crowns. Eventually in 1457, the title was conferred upon King James II's maternal half-brother, Sir John Stewart of Balvenie, ancestor of the present Atholl family.

Like the history of the family, that of the castle has been nothing if not eventful. Frequently besieged, Blair has four times been occupied by opposing forces and partly destroyed, as well as being turned from a castle into

BELOW
The Dining Room, originally a 16th-century banqueting hall, was transformed in the 18th century with magnificent plasterwork by Thomas Clayton and Thomas Bardwell.

a house and back into a castle again. King Edward III of England came to stay here in 1336; and a couple of centuries later Mary Queen of Scots was entertained to a great drive of 2,000 red deer.

By the time of Mary's visit considerable changes had taken place to the medieval castle, with the building extending southwards from Cumming's Tower. The Great Hall range, which connected the two towers, was built in about 1530 by the 3rd Earl of Atholl, who was celebrated for his hospitality. His son, the 4th Earl, Mary's host, is supposed to have been poisoned, whereas the 4th Earl's Countess was thought to possess powers of incantation.

During the Civil War John Murray, Master of Tullibardine, who acquired the Earldom of Atholl through his mother, heiress of the 5th Earl of the Stewart line, was an ardent Royalist and raised 1,800 men to support King Charles I. The dashing Cavalier Marquess of Montrose hoisted his standard at Blair in 1644. But eventually, eight years later, the castle was captured and held by Cromwell's troops until the Restoration of King Charles II.

The Athollmen who had rallied behind Montrose in 1644, however, were not to be found at the nearby Battle of Killiecrankie in 1689 when 'Bonnie' Dundee made his last stand for King James against the Dutch usurper, William of Orange. The reason was that the 1st Marquess of Atholl played, to quote *The Complete Peerage* 'a trimming and shuffling part' in the so-called 'Glorious Revolution. And so the 2nd Marquess of Atholl duly became the 1st Duke of Atholl. Nonetheless, three of his sons came out in favour of the Jacobite cause in the abortive 1715 Rising.

The divided loyalties of the Murrays were even more notable in the '45 when first Bonnie Prince Charlie stayed at Blair and then Lord George Murray, at the head of his Jacobite 'Atholl Brigade', went so far as to lay siege to the family seat, which was then occupied by Hanoverian troops. In the process, Blair gained the distinction of being the last castle in the British Isles to be besieged.

The Government-supporting 2nd Duke of Atholl was not actually inside Blair when his brother, Lord George, was bombarding the place. Once peace was resumed, this Whig grandee was able to concentrate on a dozen years of remarkable architectural achievement, which were to witness the transformation of Blair from an antiquated castle to a modern country house set in an English-style park. With the help of the architect James Winter, the old turrets and gables were removed, sash windows were installed, marble chimneypieces and new furniture shipped up from London. Even the staircase, constructed in London by a carpenter called Abraham Swan, or Swain, was transported in sections to the Highlands.

This robust Picture Staircase (grained in the 19th century) rises dramatically through three storeys. At the top, under the castle roof, is the majestic Drawing Room, hung with crimson damask and boasting a coved and richly plastered ceiling. On the floor below, the delicious green and white Dining Room is decorated with the most exuberant of Clayton's plasterwork. There is more flamboyant spectacle in the Tapestry Room, which is dominated by a late 17th-century State Bed complete with a canopy crowned by four outrageous tufts of ostrich feathers.

Altogether more than 30 rooms, culminating in the vast 1877 Ballroom, can be seen on the public tour at Blair. Not for nothing has Blair Castle been nicknamed 'the Highland Victoria & Albert'. The range of furniture, from early oak to Regency cabinets, is certainly of museum standard.

The Highland Revival found its full expression at Blair in the time of the 7th Duke of Atholl, who brought in Bryce to make it a castle once

ABOVE
The view from the 'high road': Blair Castle and the village of Blair Atholl set in the wide Strath of Garry.

more. The two main towers were built up and capped with battlements and 'pepper-pot' turrets, another tower was added to form the new entrance and turreted wings were run out to the north and south. Fortunately, though, the 18th-century interior remained untouched.

Happily, too, the family connection has not – contrary to misleading reports in the press following the death of 'Wee Iain', the 10th Duke of Atholl, in 1996 when the title passed to a South African kinsman – disappeared from the castle. Somehow, Blair – despite the legions of visitors and the enterprising new exhibition rooms retains the atmosphere of a private house.

'Wee Iain', a shy, gentle bachelor bolstered by the Pearson fortune of his mother, a daughter of the 2nd Viscount Cowdray, managed to secure Blaies future before his untimely death by setting up a charitable trust. His half-sister, Sarah Troughton, maintains a family presence at Blair; the great ancestral acres of the Atholls are in safe hands; and the artistic and political tensions inherent in the castle have been peacefully resolved.

GLAMIS CASTLE

ANGUS

LONG before Lady Elizabeth Bowes Lyon (later Queen Elizabeth The
Queen Mother) married the future King George VI, the Earls of Strathmore
were one of the most famous of the great families of Scotland, on account
of their colourful history and the bloodcurdling legends associated with
their ancestral seat of Glamis. With its massive tower and cluster of pointed
turrets, Glamis could be said to be everybody's idea of a Scottish castle,
yet in architectural terms this amazing pink apparition at the climax of a
wide avenue of oaks is remarkably unusual.

And for all its medieval core and castellated facade, Glamis is also unde-
niably a 'great house', with glorious 17th-century plasterwork and furniture,
as well as almost untouched, and highly atmospheric 19th-century decoration. Indeed, when it comes to atmosphere Glamis is surely in a class of its
own. Although the Shakespearean associations are purely fanciful, there is
good authority that King Malcolm II met his death at Glamis in 1034.

Glamis was then a royal hunting lodge and so it remained until the 14th
century when Robert II, the first Stuart King of Scots, granted the Thaneage
of Glamis to Sir John Lyon of Forteviot in 1372. 'The White Lyon', as
he was known, went on to marry the King's daughter, Princess Jean, or
'Joanna', four years later and to be appointed Chamberlain of Scotland.

It was the White Lyon's son, also Sir John, who began building the
east wing of the present castle in the early 15th century. In the next generation the 1st Lord Glamis began work on the Great Tower in about 1435.
This was completed by his widow, though it was not linked to the east wing
for a further hundred years.

In the 16th century another widow of a subsequent Lord Glamis,
the 6th, was to play a tragic role in Glamis's history. Poor Janet Douglas had

the misfortune to be the sister of the Earl of Angus, whose stepson King James V determined to destroy any Douglases he could lay his hands on. In 1537 Lady Glamis and her second husband, Archibald Campbell, were duly sentenced to death on a trumped-up charge of sorcery. Campbell, attempting to escape from Edinburgh Castle, was dashed to pieces by falling rocks, and the innocent Janet, virtually blind after languishing in a dark dungeon, was burnt as a witch on Castle Hill. Her gentle spirit is said to haunt the Chapel at Glamis.

The dastardly James V declared Glamis forfeit to the Crown and helped himself to the Lyon possessions. Yet only 20 years after James's death Janet's grandson, the 8th Lord Glamis, was entertaining the King's daughter, Mary Queen of Scots, at the castle. The 8th Lord Glamis, who was Chancellor of Scotland and Keeper of the Great Seal, had – according to the English Ambassador, who was at the party – 'the greatest revenue of any baron in Scotland'.

The family fortunes, however, were depleted by the Glamis' involvement in the Covenanting (against popery and episcopacy) troubles of the 17th century. It was said that the 2nd Earl of Kinghorne – whose father, the 9th Lord Glamis, remodelled the castle tower and stair turret and was created an Earl in 1606 – came to his inheritance the richest peer in Scotland and left it the poorest. His decision to help finance the Covenanting army resulted in debts amounting to £40,000.

The 3rd Earl (who had the designation of his peerage changed to that of 'Earl of Strathmore and Kinghorne') was advised that his estates were 'irrecoverable'. Matters were not improved by the Cromwellian occupation of Glamis. When he finally took up residence with his wife in 1670 – lodging in the only glazed rooms at the top of the great stair – prospects were bleak indeed.

Nonetheless, it is to this Lord Strathmore that Glamis owes most today. With admirable determination he managed to pay off the debts and then proceeded to remodel the castle over the next 20 years. From his *Book of Record* he emerges as a man of taste and a most sympathetic figure. It is particularly endearing to see that he kept a 'private buffoon', or jester, at Glamis – the last household to do so in Scotland. The silken suit of motley can still be seen in the Drawing Room and somehow epitomizes the zest and gaiety that outshines the ghostly gloom of the castle.

It would seem that Lord Strathmore was his own architect. In 1679 he added the west wing, and so modified the typically Scottish 'L'-shape of the old tower, and heightened the central block to give Glamis its distinctive roof-line. He placed the stone armorials on the face of the staircase tower, where his own portrait bust also appears. The avenue was laid out at an angle

of 45 degrees to the castle so that the large stair became the centre of the composition. The courtyard buildings were swept away and in front Lord Strathmore created a baroque setting of courts, sculptures and vistas.

Inside, he cleverly transformed 'My Great Hall, which is a room that I ever loved' into the delightful barrel-vaulted Drawing Room, preserving the handsome plasterwork installed in 1621 by his father, the 2nd Earl of Kinghorne. The pretty pink walls are hung with family portraits, dominated by a group study of Lord Strathmore (in a curious 'see-through' tunic) with his sons and dogs.

Another fine interior created by the 3rd Earl is the Chapel, consecrated in 1688, a fascinating survival of a decorative scheme from the time of Archbishop Laud. Both ceiling and walls are copiously covered by panels painted by the Dutch artist Jacob de Wet, depicting the Life of Christ and the Twelve Apostles.

In 1716 – the year after the first Jacobite Rising, in which the young 5th Earl of Strathmore was killed at Sheriffmuir while fighting for the Stuart cause – 'the Old Chevalier', otherwise King James VIII and III, 'touched' for the King's Evil in this chapel. That is to say, he laid hands on local sufferers from a lymphatic disorder, all of whom – so it is said – promptly recovered.

The Old Chevalier left behind a couple of items at Glamis – one deliberately, the other accidentally. His sword can be seen in the Family Exhibition, as now can the other object, a watch inadvertently forgotten under the Old Chevalier's pillow. The story goes that a maid stole it but many years later the light-fingered one's descendant returned the timepiece to Glamis.

There are also to be found diverting memorabilia in the Billiard Room, one of the improvements added by the 9th Earl of Strathmore. This Earl effectively restored the family fortunes by marrying the rich Durham heiress Mary Eleanor Bowes. The 10th Earl lived mainly on his Durham estates – his illegitimate son, John Bowes, founded the Bowes Museum at Barnard Castle – but carried on his father's improvements at Glamis, including the rebuilding of the west wing. This wing contains the impressively 'Jacobethan' Dining Room: a stately 19th-century ensemble of heraldically embossed ceiling, chimneypiece and dado, armorial glass and even fire-dogs.

The castle was modernized again at the end of the 19th century by the 13th Earl of Strathmore (whose Pinetum in the policies has itself recently been restored). In the next generation, the 14th Earl's brood of nine surviving children are evocatively portrayed in an exquisitely Edwardian conversation piece on an easel in the corner of the Drawing Room. The youngest, Lady Elizabeth, prophetically known as 'Princess', enchanted the wounded soldiers convalescing at Glamis during the First World War when her mother, Lady Strathmore, turned the castle into a hospital.

OPPOSITE
'My great hall which is a room that I have ever loved', wrote the 3rd Earl of Strathmore, portrayed in Classical costume by the prolific Jacob de Wet in the conversation piece which dominates the far end of what is now the Drawing Room. The castle's finest 17th-century interior, it has a barrel-vaulted ceiling and an armorial overmantel. The modern wooden screen, to the left, is by Viscount Linley, whose mother, Princess Margaret, was born at Glamis in 1930.

The Queen Mother's presence is particularly potent in the Royal Apartments at Glamis, which were set aside for her use by her mother in 1923 following her marriage to the Duke of York. The consummately cosy corner sitting room contains childhood photographs of the two Princesses, Elizabeth and Margaret – who was born at Glamis in 1930. Princess Margaret's craftsman son, Viscount Linley, executed the ambitious marquetry screen depicting the castle in various woods which is now a feature of the Drawing Room. Such a modern touch is a pleasing reminder that Glamis is still very much a vital, breathing family home. Lord Linley's cousin and near-contemporary, the 18th and present Earl of Strathmore and Kinghorne, still lives here with his wife and young family.

LEFT
The sideboard alcove
of the Victorian Dining
Room with portraits
of the 13th Earl of
Strathmore and his
Countess (the former
Frances Smith).

RIGHT
The Biblical scenes on
the ceiling panels of the
Chapel, by Jacob de
Wet, are thought to
have been based on
engravings by Boetius
a Bolswert, dated 1622.
De Wet's brief was to
conform to scenes in the
3rd Earl of Strathmore's
Bible – the Flight into
Egypt, the Last Supper,
and so on.

Despite the unbeatable historic allure of Glamis, it is the friendly spirit generated by recent generations of the Bowes Lyon family that makes the strongest impression amid the baronial baroque. The title of the sheet music on the piano in the Billiard Room sets the tone of the place – 'Just Snap Your Fingers at Dull Care' – conjuring up paradisial images of the centenarian Queen Mother's favourite author, P.G. Wodehouse.

DRUMLANRIG CASTLE

DUMFRIESSHIRE

THANKS to Mel Gibson's colourful, if – to say the least – historically unreliable, film, the romantic phrase 'Brave Heart' has recently rung around the world as a symbol of Scotland. In reality, or at least much better-founded tradition, the symbolism is rooted in the story of Sir James Douglas, 'The Good' or 'Black Douglas', a stalwart supporter of King Robert Bruce in the early 14th century. Robert Bruce died, in 1329, before he could go on Crusade to the Holy Land so the Black Douglas was entrusted with the King's heart. As Douglas fell mortally wounded in a battle with the Moors in Spain he is said to have hurled the royal heart (contained in a silver casket) before him with the truly epic cry: 'Forward, brave heart!'

The Douglas crest duly became a winged heart surmounted by Bruce's crown and it is this heraldic emblem that constantly catches the eye on a visit to the spectacular family seat of Drumlanrig Castle, home of the 9th Duke of Buccleuch and 11th Duke of Queensberry. The 'brave heart' (together with the motto, 'Forward') is everywhere: in stone, lead, iron, wood, leather, carpeting and so forth.

The romance needs no Hollywood burnish for surely there can be few more romantic places in the world than Drumlanrig in its dramatic Border landscape glowing pink in the twilight. Framed by skilfully planted woods and surrounded by the glorious green slopes of Nithsdale, the castle cries out for the brush of, say, Claude – one of the few great masters not to be represented on the walls within. No amount of anticipation can prepare one for the impact experienced at the climax of the ingeniously devised approach.

Facing you is a noble façade of late-Stuart Baroque which almost outdoes (and pre-dates) Sir John Vanbrugh for sheer splendour and exuberance. The eye feasts on a curving perron, an arcaded loggia, giant

PRECEDING PAGES
View of Drumlanrig
Castle from Mount
Malloch.

LEFT
View through the
Drawing Room, showing
Grinling Gibbons's
carving above the door.

RIGHT
Staircase Hall: the oak
staircase and balustrade
was one of the first of its
kind in Scotland.

pilasters, balustrades and rows of pedimented windows, and soars upwards to savour the cluster of turrets decorating the four corner towers. Then you find yourself focusing on the exquisitely adorned porch with its trophies and coats of arms.

Yet the overall effect is surprisingly simple and straightforward. The plan, after all, derives from the castles of the later Middle Ages. Indeed traces of the original Douglas stronghold dating from the 14th and 15th centuries are still discernible and the present great house – one of the foremost Renaissance buildings in the grand manner in Scottish domestic architecture – was effectively superimposed on the old castle.

The Barony of Drumlanrig was originally a property of the Earls of Mar, whose heiress had married the 1st Earl of Douglas, progenitor of a powerful Lowland dynasty whose landholdings were to stretch over much of Scotland by the end of the 14th century. The 2nd Earl of Douglas (and Mar), who was killed at the Battle of Otterburn in 1388, had a natural son, William, to whom he bequeathed Drumlanrig. Son succeeded father in the Douglas male line at Drumlanrig for nearly 400 years.

When King James VI and I was entertained at Drumlanrig in 1617, the laird of the day, Sir William Douglas, could take satisfaction from the old saw, 'He who stands on the Hassock hill/Shall rule all Nithsdale at his will'. Sir William rose to become Viscount Drumlanrig and, in 1633, Earl of Queensberry; in his grandson's time the Douglases of Drumlanrig advanced still further, to a Dukedom.

The 3rd Earl and 1st Duke of Queensberry continued the family's staunch adherence to the House of Stuart, even though his own religious views were Episcopalian while those of Kings Charles II and James VII and II veered towards Roman Catholicism. As Lord High Treasurer of Scotland, Duke William became the most powerful man in the country and decided that his family needed a more fitting pile than the old castle in which James VI had been fêted on his return to Scotland.

A man of artistic tastes, Duke William is said, as *The Complete Peerage* notes, to have 'well-nigh ruined himself' in his ambitious rebuilding operations between 1679 and 1691. His architect is not known for certain, though the most likely candidate seems to be James Smith, son-in-law of Robert Mylne, the King's Master Mason. The master of works, or builder, is, however, on record: William Lukup (buried in the nearby Durisdeer Church).

Whoever was responsible for the designs of the new Drumlanrig must have had access to the drawings made earlier in the 17th century when a remodelling of the old castle was first contemplated. (Sir William Bruce, the great gentleman amateur, was the architect consulted then.) Built of local pink sandstone, Duke William's house was constructed round an open courtyard, with a circular staircase tower in each corner. Two Dutchmen, Peter Paul Boyse and Cornelius Van Nerven, carried out the elaborate stone carving. Inside, there was the innovation of a passage linking rooms, while the magnificent oak staircase and balustrade was one of the first of its kind in Scotland. The fine wooden overmantels and overdoors are thought to be by Grinling Gibbons.

In short, no expense was spared, not forgetting the laying-out of elaborate formal gardens. Duke William came to regret his extravagance. Sir Walter Scott relates that the Duke folded up the accounts of Drumlanrig in

LEFT
A corner of the Drawing Room, showing the cabinet made for Louis XIV's Versailles and a full-length portrait of King James VI's Queen, Anne of Denmark, attributed to George Jamesone.

a sealed parcel, with a label bidding 'the deil pike out the een of any of my successors that shall open it'. Today, though, one can only salute his memory.

A less respectful gesture would be required for the 4th Duke of Queensberry – the notorious rake 'Old Q' or 'the Goat of Piccadilly' – in whose absence the Drumlanrig estate disgracefully declined. Upon Old Q's death in 1810, the Dukedom and the Marquessate of Queensberry went in different directions. The Dukedom passed to the 3rd Duke of Buccleuch, while the Marquessate was inherited by a Douglas kinsman, great-uncle of Oscar Wilde's 'Screaming Scarlet Marquess', and Old Q's cash (derived from the sale of Drumlanrig's trees) went to his illegitimate daughter, who married the 3rd Marquess of Hertford – thereby helping to fund the Wallace Collection.

The 3rd Duke of Buccleuch – a descendant of the dashing Duke of Monmouth (King Charles II's son by Lucy Walters) who married the heiress

BELOW
Bonnie Prince Charlie's Bedroom, occupied by Prince Charles Edward, 'the Young Pretender', on his retreat north on December 22, 1745. His supporters showed their dislike for King William III by lacerating his equestrian portrait in the Staircase Hall. The tapestries on the wall are late 17th-century Brussels.

ABOVE
Drawing Room, with
Grinling Gibbons's
carvings.

of the long-established Border family, the Scotts of Buccleuch – not only came into the Douglas Dukedom of Queensberry and the Drumlanrig estate but also married the eventual heiress of the English Dukes of Montagu. Consequently Drumlanrig's contents were enhanced by the combined treasures of the Montagus and Scotts, on top of those of the Douglases.

The 4th Duke of Buccleuch (and 6th Duke of Queensberry) inherited the Drumlanrig estate in 1812 and embarked on an ambitious programme to repair the depredations wrought by Old Q, with copious advice from his friend and kinsman Sir Walter Scott. His son, Walter Francis, succeeded him seven years later, at the age of 12. As 5th Duke, he proved to be a public-spirited agriculturalist and philanthropist, who replanted woodlands, modernized farmsteads and transformed Drumlanrig into the thriving rural estate it remains today.

To bring the story up to date, a 20-year programme of renewing all the lead roofing, including the rebuilding of all the little cupolas, was

completed in 1995 without, as the present Duke points out, any Government grants. The repair and replacement of the stone carvings, some of which had crumbled away beyond recognition, are well advanced but at least another ten years will be needed. The pace of progress depends upon the estate's farms and forests continuing to provide the necessary finance despite such setbacks as BSE and fluctuating timber prices. This, as the Duke says, 'demonstrates the importance of the cohesion between an historic house and its surrounding countryside'.

The fabulous treasures of Drumlanrig would soon exhaust descriptive superlatives. A remark made by the present Duke of Buccleuch as he showed us round speaks volumes: 'If you lie on your back underneath the 1670s silver chandelier on the staircase,' he encouraged the photographer, 'it must be the only place in the world where you can see simultaneously a Rembrandt, a Holbein and a Leonardo da Vinci.'

The plethora of family portraits are brought up to date by a charming 1950s study of the present Duchess by John Merton in the Morning Room. This is a reminder that Drumlanrig is still a much-loved family home at the centre of a flourishing community, rightly celebrated for its contributions to countryside management and education. The conservationist Dr David Bellamy has described the Duke's property as 'the best-managed estates in the world'.

LEFT
Roofscape, in light and shade.

RIGHT
The Duke of Buccleuch at Drumlanrig.

CAWDOR CASTLE

NAIRN

THE familiar Shakespearean quotation 'This castle hath a pleasant seat...' tends to be bandied about in association with Cawdor Castle. Yet, as the late Earl Cawdor pointed out in his witty guide-book to the castle – surely the most entertaining and instructive example of that often dismally dull genre – Macbeth himself died in 1052 whereas the 1st Thane of Cawdor did not flourish until the end of the 13th century.

'The truth is', Hugh Cawdor wrote, 'that as Cawdor Castle was not built until the late 14th century, it is impossible for King Duncan to have lost any blood or Lady Macbeth much sleep in this house.' One can sympathize with the exasperated explanation of the 5th Earl (Hugh's father): 'I wish the Bard had never written his damned play.'

Nonetheless, haunting Shakespearean overtones somehow cling to this atmospheric castle, with its great medieval tower and old drawbridge (the only one extant at a privately inhabited castle in Scotland), brooding above dark Cawdor burn. Paradoxically, though, the castle is also far from a fortress in character: it is a great house of intimacy and charm surrounded by delightful gardens and serene parkland. In architectural terms it is a perfect instance of a Scots 'compound' great house: 14th-century great keep, 15th-century fortifications; 17th-century domestic additions.

Even if the *Macbeth* legend does not – to borrow one of Hugh Cawdor's colourful phrases – 'hold Scotch mist, let alone water', the tradition of the castle's building is inevitably romantic. The story goes that the 3rd Thane of Cawdor, who had a small castle about a mile away, decided to build a stronger tower on a higher site and that this new situation was chosen not by an architect but by a donkey ('creatures with much in common', as Hugh Cawdor put it). For the Thane had a dream. As instructed by his subconscious, he duly loaded a coffer of gold on to the back of a donkey and let

PRECEDING PAGES
View of the back of the
castle from the burn.

LEFT
Cleaning the grille, in
keeping with the Thanes'
family motto displayed
above the entrance
archway: 'be mindful'.

ABOVE
The Tower Room: Flemish tapestries, eclectic pictures and furniture, such as the 18th-century Venetian gondola seat in the foreground. Note the thickness of the wall in the window recess to the left. The door on the right led to a medieval closet (in the most basic sense of that euphemism).

it roam about the district for a day. The theory was that wherever the animal lay down to rest in the evening, there the Thane's castle would be sited and it would prosper for evermore. Presumably to the Thane's chagrin, the ass lay down beneath a tree.

To this day the stout central vault of the old tower boasts the astonishing sight of an ancient tree trunk. For centuries it was assumed to be a hawthorn – the vault, or ground-floor guardroom is known as the Thorn Tree Room – but in fact microscopic analysis of the wood has identified the tree as a holly.

In any event, Special Licence to fortify was granted in 1454 by King James II to his friend the 6th Thane of Cawdor, Crown Chamberlain beyond the Spey, with a significant reference to 'the perfection and completion of the said Castle [of Cawdor]'. The original tower-house – tall, plain, rectangular – would have comprised four storeys and a garret, served by a turnpike stair. There was only one entrance to the outside world set at upper

first floor level – 'the perfect design to keep out tourists' as Hugh Cawdor observes in the castle guide-book.

The present Campbells of Cawdor descend from a remarkable forced union (what Hugh Cawdor typically called a 'crossbow wedding') at the beginning of the 16th century. The greedy 2nd Earl of Argyll, the most influential man in Scotland at the time, decided to kidnap the posthumous baby daughter of his kinsman the 8th Thane of Cawdor. The wretched infant Muriel was branded on the hip with a red-hot key and the top joint of the little finger of her left hand was bitten off. In 1510, at the age of 12, Muriel was duly married to Argyll's younger son, Sir John Campbell. Curiously, the marriage worked well enough.

In due time Sir John consolidated the Cawdor estate and the subsequent Thanes became almost too powerful for their own good. The 11th Thane was blown away by a blunderbuss in a clan feud; the 12th Thane overreached himself by buying the island of Islay; and the unfortunate 13th

ABOVE
The Tapestry Bedroom, above the great hall, which was done up for the 15th Thane's marriage in 1662 to Lady Henrietta Stuart at the nearby Darnaway Castle. Their marriage-bed has been restored with crimson velvet hangings and white feathers in accordance with Lady Henrietta's housekeeping notebook of 1688. The Flemish tapestries were brought over in 1682.

Thane, 'the fiar', was certified insane, a condition possibly not unconnected with his wife's habit of poisoning the victuals. The morning after one jolly supper party at Cawdor three guests were found dead in their beds.

Happily, at last the house was put literally in order by the lunatic's nephew, Sir Hugh Campbell, the 15th Thane, who preferred to mind his own business and devote himself to the sporting pleasures of the chase. Together with his wife, Lady Henrietta Stuart (daughter of the 3rd Earl

of Moray from neighbouring Darnaway Castle), Sir Hugh succeeded in transforming the forbidding old fortress of Cawdor into a comfortable great
house between 1684 and 1702. As his descendant and namesake put it,
'Whereas his ancestors had set the castle out in such a way as to give maraud-
ers a hot reception with boiling oil and molten lead, he could now rest happily
at ease and grant his friends a warm welcome with mulled claret beside a
glowing hearth'.

The windows became larger, robust fireplaces were installed, and splendid beds and tapestries brought in. A strange little tower, which had
stood at the northeast corner of the Old Hall, was demolished; a new library
wing was added complete with a balustrade echoing the Palladian principles
of Sir Hugh's nephew, the celebrated architect Colen Campbell; and the
whole composition of the castle was neatly tidied up so that, in the words
of the building contract, the craftsmen completed everything in 'handsomest
order, so as themselves may have credit and Sir Hugh satisfaction'.

Yet in the troubled times after the first Jacobite Rising and the death
of Sir Hugh (who had nobly declared his hand for the Stuart cause) the following year, there was to be little mulled claret at Cawdor. The Thanes wisely
decamped to their Welsh estates for the next century, leaving Cawdor to the
care of factors – though in the 1720s Sir Hugh's younger son, Sir Archibald
Campbell, carried out various improvements including the creation of the
upper garden.

Neglect of an old house can be a joyful preservative. Cawdor was consequently spared the fashionable changes of the 18th century; and fortunately
the 19th century, when the Thanes returned, proved much more in sympathy with the castle's spirit. Some essential building work was necessary
after a fire in 1819 which devastated the middle storeys of the tower. The
1st Earl Cawdor first built a sturdy factor's house on the south (overlooking Sir Archibald's garden) which was subsequently extended and grafted
on to the castle itself. Then, in 1855, Sir Hugh's leaky library roof was
replaced with a pitched roof containing pedimented dormers. A balanc-
ing wing was done in the same style and on the east the flourish of a corbelled
hanging turret was added to the composition.

These 19th-century improvements were attractively in keeping,
right down to the engaging half-moon seats at the drawbridge. Indeed today's
visitor would be hard-pressed to distinguish between the authentic old
castle and the Victorian touches. The collection of tapestries at Cawdor is
outstanding – ranging from late 17th-century Arras in the Tapestry Room
depicting the Story of Noah to the slightly later Adventures of Don Quixote
(of mysterious, possibly Soho, provenance) in the Dining Room. Brussels
tapestries also adorn the Tower Room, where the pictures on display are

PRECEDING PAGES
An ancient, honourable
and agreeable seat...':
Cawdor by floodlight.
The banner of the
Campbells, Earls and
Thanes of Cawdor, flies
above the 14th-century
great keep.

characteristically eclectic – echoing Jacob Bogdoni's study of a magpie to be found here. An early Claude landscape hangs harmoniously with works by artists as varied as Stanley Spencer, John Piper and Carel Weight, as well as cartoons by Charles Addams and Salvador Dali (of Macbeth – who else?). Masterpieces sit happily beside mementoes in a gloriously unmuseum-like manner.

Family portraits are brought to invigorating life by the sparklingly irreverent descriptions in the guide-book, and in the room captions, by Hugh, the mercurial 6th Earl Cawdor who died in 1993, aged only 60. He summed up his family's history as 'good plain cooking with an occasional pinch of red pepper.

Cawdor Castle remains the cherished family home of the 6th Earl's widow, the former Countess Angelika Lazansky von Bukowa. From the tips of the turrets to the impenetrable depths of the lower garden maze beside the ambrosial mimosa, this enchanting place is still essentially very much what the 17th Thane of Cawdor described in the 18th century: an 'ancient, honourable and agreeable seat'.

DUNROBIN CASTLE

SUTHERLAND

YOU have to go a long way north to see Dunrobin Castle – it is by far the most northerly of Scotland's great houses – but the journey is abundantly worthwhile. For there can be few more amazing sights in the British Isles than the view from the sea beyond Goispie, taking in the imposing formal gardens and the terraces leading up to the fairytale palace perched on the cliff. The gloriously dotty skyline puts one in mind of 'mad' King Ludwig of Bavaria, or even Disneyland.

Yet buried underneath the 19th-century French Renaissance flourishes of Sir Charles Barry for the 2nd Duke of Sutherland is a venerable Scottish seat with the proud claim of being one of Britain's oldest continuously inhabited houses. Certainly the Earldom of Sutherland is one of Scotland's most ancient titles, dating back to about 1235. Dunrobin is mentioned in a document for the first time in 1401 as a stronghold of the family, though the core of the present building may well be older than that. Christopher Hussey considered there was 'little doubt that the keep was originally built about 1275'.

The quadrangle came into being later, and the whole was apparently 'reedified and built againe' during the reign of King Charles II, as well as being done over in the 18th century. The old harled house – which still stands, forming the west wing – appears to have had pointed towers and a row of battlements (removed during the 19th-century alterations) round the parapets.

The succession to the Earldom of Sutherland, which can pass through the female line in default of male heirs, has been the cause of considerable friction down the centuries. In the 18th century the long-drawn out 'Sutherland Peerage Case', an immensely costly affair, became a *cause célèbre*.

Judgment was eventually given by the House of Lords in favour of Elizabeth, the young daughter of the 18th Earl (whose own father had narrowly
avoided capture by the Jacobites when they briefly occupied Dunrobin in
1745). The long reign of Elizabeth – a beauty with what Byron called
'princessly manners', who was a watercolourist and correspondent of Sir
Waiter Scott – at Dunrobin effectively spanned the old world and the
new. By the time of her death in 1839 both the castle and its enormous
estates had been radically changed.

Indeed, particularly as far as the estates are concerned, 'radically' is the
mot juste. For the notorious' Highland Clearances' carried out on the Sutherland estates in the early 19th century in order to make larger and more
up-to-date agricultural holdings, and introduce sheep, were actually inspired
by progressive economic theories and reforming zeal. The irony was that
Elizabeth's husband, the 1st Duke of Sutherland, who became the bogey-
man of radical demonology, was himself a liberal of advanced views.

Shocked by the primitive conditions of his wife's tenantry, the Duke
(originally an Englishman called George Granville Leveson-Gower, who
succeeded to his father's Marquessate of Stafford and was described by
the diarist Charles Greville as 'a leviathan of wealth') consulted James Loch,
MP, a theorist in political economy from Edinburgh, concerning 'improvements'. The results, carried out with the harshness of those days by the

Duke's agents, caused terrible sufferings: 5,000 people were evicted from the glens of Sutherland. A native culture was virtually destroyed by 'progress'.

A giant statue of the 1st Duke by Sir Francis Chantrey on a mountainside outside Golspie dominates the landscape and a few agitators claim to be so upset by his looming presence that they want it pulled down. History, however, cannot be rewritten. If nothing else, the statue serves as a reminder of the dangers of do-goodery.

The 2nd Duke of Sutherland left a more universally admired memorial in the fantastic shape of the castle itself. Shortly after he succeeded to the Dukedom in 1833 he commissioned Sir Charles Barry to transform a traditional Scottish castle into a Franco-Scots extravaganza. Barry's ambitious plans took the shape of a vast triangle of buildings, with the east side of the old castle as its base, designed in a French Renaissance version of the original style, complete with dormers and steep conical roofs. The yellow sandstone used in the building operations by W. Leslie of Aberdeen

BELOW
The Green and Gold Room, done up in the French style for Duchess Eileen, wife of the 5th Duke, in 1921. The gilt four-poster (formerly in a room which is now part of the Library) was slept in by Queen Victoria on her visit to Dunrobin in 1872.

ABOVE The Drawing Room: created by Sir Robert Lorimer after the 1915 fire by throwing together two smaller rooms. The lace-like armorial ceiling, designed by Lorimer, was made by Sam Wilson in 1919. The furniture is mainly of the Louis XV period; the tapestries are Mortlake, depicting scenes from the life of Diogenes; and of the two Venetian views over the fireplaces, one is attributed to the Russian topographical master, Peter Aleksayev.

even bears a resemblance to that used on the *châteaux* of the Loire. Here is the 'Auld Alliance' with a vengeance. Inside, the sensational staircase was constructed of Caen stone (too soft for external use), brought over from France. When Barry himself came north to inspect his creation at Dunrobin in 1848 he added the imposing entrance tower as well as designing the gardens.

Unfortunately, much of Barry's work was destroyed by a fire in 1915, when the castle was being used as an auxiliary Naval hospital. Nonetheless, this has not turned out to be such a disaster as was first thought, for the architect brought in by the 5th Duke of Sutherland once the war was over, Sir Robert Lorimer, is increasingly being appreciated as one of Scotland's most accomplished and sympathetic designers. His sensitive treatment of Dunrobin's spirit has created interiors of singular charm.

Lorimer simplified and recapped Barry's entrance tower and ingeniously replanned the building inside. Two drawing rooms were knocked into one spacious, light chamber reminiscent of a long gallery. A lace-like ceiling completes a very pleasing composition.

There is another enriched ceiling in the Dining Room, though the Pompeiian-style frieze contrasts a little jarringly with the essentially 'homespun' atmosphere generated by the Scotch oak panelling. Lorimer's engaging fondness for native timbers is shown to especially good effect in the sycamore-finished Library. The 5th Duke's Duchess, Eileen, had leanings to the French taste in keeping with Dunrobin's style and she was responsible for the sumptuous Green and Gold Room.

On the death of the 5th Duke in 1963 the Dukedom of Sutherland passed to the 5th Earl of Ellesmere (a descendant of the second son of the 1st Duke of Sutherland) but the Earldom of Suther-

land carried on in the female line, being inherited, together with Dunrobin and its estates, by another Elizabeth, the present Countess. Lady Sutherland kept the castle going as a school for a time, and today her elder son, Lord Strathnaver, lives nearby with his young family and opens it to the public. The recent restoration projects have included the completion of the Pyramid Garden (with traditional Victorian plantings by the head gardener, Ian Crisp) and a re-hanging of the pictures by Alec Cobbe.

No visit to Dunrobin would be complete without calling in on the Museum in the grounds. Originally a large summerhouse, built in 1732, it was turned into a museum in 1878 by the 3rd Duke of Sutherland. The 4th Duke and his wife, Duchess Millicent, a magpie-style collector, added what could be described as the 'beachcomber' elements. Giraffes' heads jostle with elephants' trunks and rhinoceroses' tails from the bags of the 5th Duke of Sutherland, a big-game enthusiast. In short, it is surely the most remarkable personal museum in the British Isles. Wildly 'politically incorrect', it happily survives to illustrate the unfashionable truth that private ownership brings history to life far more vividly than any State organization can ever hope to achieve, and in doing so links the past to the present and future.

LEFT
Big Game Golgotha: animal trophies in the astonishing Museum.

RIGHT
View up to the terraces and the turreted ducal palace from the gardens.

TRAQUAIR HOUSE

PEEBLESSHIRE

TRAQUAIR, tucked away in the lush Tweed valley near the village of Inner-leithen, is advertised in the tourist brochures as 'The Oldest Inhabited House in Scotland'. Such claims are frequently made and difficult to establish, but in this case one is happy to accept it, along with the stirring family tradition of the Bear Gates ('the Steekit Yetts'), which were closed after Bonnie Prince Charlie's departure, never to be opened again until a Stuart King is restored to the throne. For so overwhelming is the romance of this enchanting, quintessentially Scottish seat of a nobly Catholic and Jacobite dynasty that conventional critical faculties are melted away.

The precise historical facts about Traquair – and there is a mine of material contained in the family papers – seem to matter much less than its extraordinarily eloquent spirit. The present Laird, Catherine Maxwell Stuart, expresses this point nicely when, recalling how much her father told her about Traquair's history, she says, 'Most of all I think I learnt from him to appreciate the wonderful atmosphere'. There is indeed, as she puts it, 'a tranquillity and peace that is hard to find nowadays'.

Above all, Traquair is a refreshingly friendly, unstuffy and welcoming place. Whether you are studying the evocative Stuart relics, worshipping in the Chapel, supping the potent Traquair Ale in the tea room, or blundering about in the new maze at the back of the house, you somehow feel at home. The documents on display in the Museum Room bring Traquair's history to life. Originally a hunting lodge of the Scottish Kings, its first recorded royal visit was in 1107, from King Alexander. Later in the century William 'the Lion' is said to have regarded Traquair as his favourite residence. Situated on a bend of the River Tweed, Traquair would have occupied a strong strategic position during the years of Border warfare.

As you look at the main front of the house today – solid, harled, dormered
and steeply pitched – it is not immediately apparent which generation was
responsible for which bit of building. The oldest part of the house, to the
left, has the remains of a Pele tower with narrow newel staircase.

Eventually, after numerous changes of ownership, Traquair was granted
in 1469 by King James III to his current favourite, William Rogers, who was
described as 'Master of Music'. Then, nine years later, a curious transac-
tion took place, as recorded in the Museum Room. Rogers sold Traquair
and all its lands to the King's uncle, 'Hearty James', Earl of Buchan, for
the paltry sum of 70 Scots merks (£3.15s.10d) – to be paid in two instal-
ments. Peter Maxwell Stuart, 20th Laird of Traquair, described this in
his history of the house as 'one of the most remarkable deeds of sale in
history'. Presumably the document was drawn up under duress, for when
Hearty James's far from hearty nephew King James III was absent abroad
in 1482, Hearty James and his cronies lost no time in stringing Rogers
up from Lauder Bridge.

Hearty James had his eye on Traquair as a handy property for his second son, James Stuart, who duly became the 1st Laird of the present line of owners. The charter of 1491 confirming him in possession describes the *'turris et fortalicis de Trakware'*. James's plans to extend the building came to nought when he was killed at the Battle of Flodden.

His son William, the 2nd Laird, made various additions: for example, the remarkably early mural painting in the Museum Room, which shows birds, beasts and vines bordered by scriptural texts, probably dates from this time, *circa* 1530. This was discovered at the beginning of the 20th century under a covering of wallpaper.

The 5th Laird, Sir William Stuart, a courtier of King James VI, left his initials on a window lintel on the west front of Traquair, commemorating the building improvements carried out in 1599. More substantial alterations were made during the time of the 7th Laird, who was created Earl of Traquair in 1633 by King Charles I. The new young Lord Traquair rose rapidly to become Lord High Treasurer of Scotland and the most powerful man in Scotland after the King, but he became unstuck amid the fierce religious differences of that turbulent period. His fall in 1641 and confinement to his estates, however, were to have a beneficial effect on Traquair itself.

RIGHT
Staircase landing.

LEFT
Traquair: quintessentially
Scottish.

Besides changing the course of the Tweed away from the house, he added an extra storey and, by regularizing – to a degree – the fenestration, left the main part of the building looking very much as it does today. Almost the only decorative feature outside is the series of pedimented dormer windows in the steep roof and the little corner turrets, which both reflect the French influence.

After the death in 1659 of 'the Beggar Earl', Traquair became a bastion of Catholicism when his son, the 2nd Earl, embraced the Old Faith. He married two Catholic wives in succession, and the concealed staircase (at the back of a cupboard in the room at the top of the house where Mass was celebrated) probably dates from the time of the second wife, Lady Anne Seton. It provided a quick escape route for priests during the Penal era when the house was searched. In 1688, the year of the so-called 'Glorious Revolution', a Presbyterian mob from Peebles ransacked Traquair and destroyed all the 'Popish Trinkets' they could find.

Traquair also became a stronghold of Jacobitism as well as of Catholicism. The 4th Earl was imprisoned in Edinburgh Castle at the time of the 1715 Rising. His Countess, the beautiful daughter of the 4th Earl of Nithsdale, fully shared his commitment to the cause. The widow of the 20th Laird, Flora Maxwell Stuart, paints a vivid picture of the perils of such loyalty in her book *Lady Nithsdale and the Jacobites*, which tells of how Lady Traquair's sister-in-law courageously rescued her husband from the Tower of London.

The 4th Earl added the two wings and the wrought-iron railings which brought about the composition of a forecourt to give an air of formality to Traquair's entrance front. This was enhanced by the long avenue he

RIGHT
Still going strong:
Traquair's Ales take
pride of place on an
old dresser.

also planted. At the back he added a terrace, ending in two little domed pavilions, and created a formal garden, where the maze now stands.

The 5th Earl of Traquair managed to tickle up the interior after his release from the Tower of London, where he was sentenced to two years for his part in the 1745 Rising. Local artists were brought in to paint the panels over the doors and fireplaces.

The Earldom of Traquair expired in 1861 with the death of the 8th Earl, an engagingly eccentric bachelor whose passions were sharpening razors and hunting wasps. He became so fed up with his family's efforts at match-making that he deterred potential brides by placing stinging nettles in their beds.

ABOVE
The King's Room, in the original part of Traquair, where Mary Queen of Scots stayed in 1566. The State Bed, remodelled in the 18th century, was brought from Terregles House. The hand-stitched quilt is said to have been worked by the Queen and her ladies-in-waiting.

The estate, which the 8th and last Earl had modernized, passed to his redoubtable spinster sister, Lady Louise Stuart, who lived to nearly 100. Next, Traquair was inherited by her kinsman Henry Constable Maxwell (who duly took the surname of Stuart), brother of the 10th Lord Herries and a descendant of the Jacobite Earl of Nithsdale as well as of the 4th Earl of Traquair.

Freed from anti-Catholic restrictions, the family resumed service to their country: no less than four Maxwell Stuart boys were killed in action or died of wounds between 1916 and 1918, as recorded in the Chapel (converted from an old storeroom above the Brew House). The Brew House itself was revived by Peter Maxwell Stuart, the 20th Laird, and continues to thrive as the demand for traditional 'real ales' grows ever stronger.

Peter's parents, who came to live at Traquair during the Second World War following the deaths of two bachelor Lairds, did much to restore the place and to bring it into the modern world (electricity was eventually installed in the 1950s). They opened Traquair to the public and Peter, in turn, dedicated himself to its development and preservation until his death in 1990.

His widow and daughter have carried on the good work. For all the peace and serenity, Traquair buzzes with life. Not for nothing did the great chronicler of Borders life, Sir Walter Scott, find inspiration for the 'House of Tullyveolan', the 'Bears of Bradwarline' and 'Shaw's Castle' in this supremely Scottish shrine of the Stuarts.

RIGHT
The Bear Gates ('Steekit Yetts'), built in 1737–8 for the 4th Earl of Traquair, and closed after Bonnie Prince Charlie's visit in 1745 – never to be opened again until a Stuart King is crowned in London.

THIRLESTANE CASTLE

BERWICKSHIRE

BESIDES being a thrilling piece of architecture – a huge sandstone castle built on a 'T'-plan with an ingenious cluster of turrets and pinnacles – Thirlestane, set in wooded parkland above the Border town of Lauder, has a special significance for everyone interested in heritage matters. For its ownership has set an encouraging precedent for the survival of such places as family homes rather than as bureaucratically-run museums.

In 1984 Captain Gerald ('Bunny') Maitland-Carew, who had inherited Thirlestane Castle a dozen years earlier from his maternal grandmother, the Countess of Lauderdale (widow of the 15th Earl), gave the main part of this great building, together with its contents, to a charitable trust set up for its preservation, which was then endowed by the National Heritage Memorial Fund. This partnership between the public and private sector came to be known as the 'Thirlestane Formula'. It has since been put into practice at several other historic houses – including Paxton, also in Berwickshire – and provides an alternative to the often prohibitively expensive 'safety nets' of the National Trusts for troubled family seats.

The trouble with Thirlestane when Bunny Maitland-Carew and his wife Rosalind came to live at the castle in 1972 was basically dry rot. No fewer than 40 serious outbreaks of dry rot demanded attention and the massive central tower was leaning alarmingly backwards. With the help of grants from the Historic Buildings Council a phenomenal programme of work was carried out: new steel support beams were installed, the stonework was extensively rebuilt, timbers replaced, the famously ornate ceilings repaired, the principal rooms completely redecorated.

On show in the castle is a display recording the detail of the rescue operation, with some startling 'before' and 'after' photographs. The exhi-

PRECEDING PAGES
Borders roofscape.

ABOVE
The Entrance Front, with its grand staircase.

bition also helps to clarify Thirlestane's complex architectural history. Essentially, what we see today is the result of three periods of building: the 1590s, the 1670s and the 1840s.

The first stage was the responsibility of John Maitland, Lord Chancellor of Scotland and the 1st Lord Maitland of Thirlestane. His elder brother, William, celebrated as Mary Queen of Scots's Secretary of State, had inherited the principal family seat of Lethington Castle (now called Lennoxlove, and the home of the Dukes of Hamilton) in East Lothian, but John, having established himself in his own right, determined to build a pile befitting his powerful status.

The Thirlestane estate had been in the Maitland family since the mid-13th century. With its prominent position overlooking Leader Water some 28 miles south-east of Edinburgh, it was strategically placed to defend the city from the south. A large Border fort occupied the site chosen by Chancellor Maitland for his new keep. The keep forms the stem of the 'T'-shape of Thirlestane, and was at the time of its construction in the 1590s considered remarkable for its symmetry, with four large corner towers along its flanks.

The second stage in the building of Thirlestane came about on the creation of the 2nd Earl of Lauderdale (the Chancellor's grandson) as Duke of Lauderdale in 1672. A colourful and controversial character, the Duke is known to history as the 'L' in King Charles II's 'Cabal' administration. His estates had been sequestrated by the Cromwellians after he was taken prisoner at the Battle of Worcester in 1651 and he languished for nine years in the Tower of London, but he bounced back at the Restoration of Charles II, who made him his Secretary of State for Scotland. As virtually the uncrowned 'King' of Scotland Lauderdale wielded enormous power, especially following his second marriage to the haughty heiress of Ham House in Surrey, the Countess of Dysart, when he was granted a Dukedom. He decided to make a sensational splash at Thirlestane.

Inside, the Duke ordered the State Rooms to be of as 'fine worke as possible'. The English plasterer George Dunsterfield obliged with an amazing series of immensely rich and elaborate ceilings. The gloriously lush and robust plasterwork, bursting with the confident exuberance of the Carolean Age, is undoubtedly the highlight of a visit to Thirlestane. Look up and you will see a cornucopia of garlanded flowers, leaves, grapes and the Lauderdale heraldic eagles.

The Duke's architect for the lavish remodelling was Sir William Bruce, master of the Scottish Renaissance. Bruce's satisfying sense of 'mass' in a building is splendidly exemplified at Thirlestane. His genius enabled the palace that the irrepressible Duke craved to retain the feeling of a castle. He

LEFT
Detail of George
Dunsterfield's
plasterwork, notable for
its deep relief. He
worked at the castle from
1674 to 1676 and is
thought to have been
inspired by the Italian
Renaissance artist Andrea
Mantegna.

BELOW LEFT
The ubiquitous
Lauderdale eagle (which
supports the Maitland
coat-of-arms) at the foot
of an elaborate gilded
drawing-room mirror.

RIGHT
The Dining Room, in the
south wing added by
William Burn and David
Bryce in the 1840s. The
Jacobean-style ceiling is
by James Annan and is
thought to have been
based on the oldest
surviving ceiling in the
house of *circa* 1590. The
dining chairs were made
for the Duchess of
Richmond's Ball on the
eve of Waterloo. Among
the fine collection of
family portraits is the
Duke of Lauderdale
above the fireplace.

planned the construction of the two new front towers and the grand
staircase, which together dominate the approach to the castle. The dramatic
composition of the entrance reflects the Restoration love of spectacle and
pomp. No one could ride up to the front door; all had to dismount at the
foot of the broad flight of steps before the grand terrace.

All this grandeur appears to have gone to the Duke's already large head.

He has certainly received a mixed press from his contemporaries and from historians. Lord Clarendon observed that Lauderdale was 'insolent, imperious, flattering and dissembling, and having no impediment of honour to restrain him from doing anything that might satisfy any of his passions'. Yet, for all his faults, it is difficult not to warm to this larger-than-life character, memorably described by Bishop Burnet as 'very big, his hair red, hanging oddly about him; his tongue was too big for his mouth

which made him bedew all that he talked to'. Greedy and crude, he was prone to gobble a leg of lamb before going out to dinner and, hardly surprisingly, was a martyr to indigestion. He would complain, in his broad Scots brogue, that the pain in his stomach was 'closer to my arse than my jewels'. At Court he joshed the Bishop of London 'Your Grace, you're snoring so loudly that you'll wake the King'.

Eventually, though, the King was wide enough awake, under pressure from a united front of his administration, to sack the Duke from all his offices. The Dukedom of Lauderdale died with him in 1682, but the Earldom and the Thirlestane estate passed to his brother, Charles.

Thirlestane ceased to be at the hub of national affairs and settled into a more domestic establishment noted for its sporting house parties. So popular had these become by the dawn of the Victorian Age that the newly inherited 9th Earl of Lauderdale commissioned the Edinburgh architect David Bryce in 1840 to create more space at the castle. Fortunately Bryce was an admirer of Bruce's work at Thirlestane in the 1670s and his additions were broadly in sympathy with his predecessor's, though the stonework is noticeably darker than the creamy tones of the central keep.

Two large wings were built on to this keep, the south wing being constructed around a central courtyard and containing a 'Jacobean'-style dining room, new kitchens, pantries, laundries and staff bedrooms. Bryce gave the wings towers to match the outer towers of the original keep and could not resist raising the central tower which he crowned with an ogee roof flanked by a series of turrets. The result was a highly spectacular skyline.

Today the Maitland-Carews live in the north wing, and the south wing is given over to the Border Country Life Museum, a skilful evocation of the activities on and around the country estate. The horse naturally looms large in the exhibition, for Captain Maitland-Carew, who won the Grand Military Cup at Sandown Park in 1968 and is a member of the Jockey Club, holds the Scottish Championship Horse Trials on the estate.

The old nurseries house a nostalgic collection of old toys and Captain Maitland-Carew has created a very jolly print room, in tribute to the celebrated one at his paternal home of Castletown in County Kildare. Recently the Duke of Lauderdale's Grand Bedchamber has been reinstated in what was previously called the Red Drawing Room.

RIGHT
Looking through from the Ante-Drawing Room to the Long Drawing Room. The swan-pedimented doorcases in the Ante-Drawing Room recall those supplied by the joiner Thomas Carter at Ham House in Surrey in 1639; Sir William Bruce is known to have used two German craftsmen who had worked at Ham to carry out this joinery, which evokes the fantastic palaces found east of the Rhine.

SCONE PALACE

PERTHSHIRE

THE Moot Hill, or 'Hill of Credulity', that rises a hundred yards north of the present Scone Palace – seat of the Murrays, Earls of Mansfield, since 1604 – has been aptly described as 'the heart of the Scottish Kingdom'. Made of earth from all parts of the realm, it has witnessed the early councils of the Pictish Kings; the embracing in the 8th century by King Nectan of 'the customs of the Church of Rome'; and possibly even the ingenious sabotaging of the Picts by Kenneth MacAlpin in AD 835. The story goes that Kenneth, King of the Scots, while entertaining the Pictish King Drostan and his nobles, took advantage of 'their perhaps excessive gluttony' by tipping them up inside the benches they had imagined they had been sitting on. Caught in a trap, the Picts were swiftly put to the sword.

After Scone became an Augustinian abbey it continued to be the fount of Scots law. Councils and Parliaments were held at Scone and the great bell would sound before the promulgation of any new law. The Abbey came to an undignified end in the Reformation when, in 1559, a Presbyterian mob inflamed by the rantings of John Knox destroyed the place.

The remnants of the ancient 'Royal City' and the monastery were given to the Ruthvens, Earls of Gowrie, who built themselves a gabled house on the ruins in about 1580. Twenty years later, though, they became unstuck through the 'Gowrie Conspiracy', a mysterious attempt to kidnap King James VI (with whom the Ruthvens had a long-running feud).

So King James decided to grant Scone to someone he could trust with such a precious heritage, Sir David Murray, one of his most stalwart supporters at the time of the Gowrie Conspiracy. Murray, who filled the offices of the King's Ceremonial Cup Bearer, Master of the Horse, Comptroller of Scotland and Captain of the King's Guard, was created Lord Scone in 1604.

PRECEDING PAGES
The east (entrance) front
framed in the arch of the
early 17th-century
Gatehouse.

LEFT
The Royal Long Gallery
– and it is unusually long
for a Scottish house –
142 feet, in fact. As for
the 'Royal' connotations,
King Charles II walked
down the gallery *en route*
for his Coronation at
Moot Hill in the
grounds; and Queen
Victoria and Prince
Albert were given a
demonstration of the
principles of curling on
the polished floor
(Scottish oak inset with
bog oak). The chairs are
Chinese Chippendale.

In about 1618 Lord Scone appears to have built two principal ranges of the Palace facing south and east. The east range contained the Long Gallery, which had a painted ceiling. The picturesque gatehouse, which frames the present east front at Scone, also dates from the early 17th century. The most striking relic from this period which survives at Scone, though, is the magnificent memorial to Lord Scone, or the 1st Viscount of Stormont as he became in 1621, ten years before his death. The sumptuously carved monument in Italian alabaster was executed by Maximilian Colt in 1618/19 in London and sent north.

LEFT
A range and copper pots
in the Old Kitchen. The
room is now used as a
restaurant for visitors.

It was in the time of the 3rd Viscount Stormont that King Charles II came to stay in the Palace and was crowned King of Scots on the Moot Hill on New Year's Day 1651 – the only purely Presbyterian Coronation that has ever taken place. Unfortunately, the proceedings were rather marred by the long-windedness of the Moderator of the General Assembly of the Church of Scotland, who addressed the congregation for an hour and a half.

There were more royal visitors in the 18th century, when the Old Chevalier and Bonnie Prince Charlie were entertained at Scone during the 1715 and 1745 Jacobite Risings respectively. Their hosts, the 5th and 6th Viscounts Stormont, were both imprisoned for their pains and had to go into exile.

Among the treasures in the Palace, hanging in the present Drawing Room is Sir Joshua Reynolds's portrait of the most eminent member of the Murray family, the 1st Earl of Mansfield, twice Lord Chief Justice and Chancellor of the Exchequer. 'Sir Joshua himself', wrote Lord Mansfield of the portrait, 'thinks it one of the best he ever did.' In it, we see the great jurist seated and looking wonderfully wise and benign.

Although it would have been appropriate for possibly the finest lawyer of all time to be seated in a palace steeped in the legal traditions of his native land, William was only a younger son and had to content himself with employing another great Scot, Robert Adam, to remodel his Hampstead residence,

Kenwood House. Scone itself was inherited by his nephew, the 7th Viscount Stormont, a brilliant diplomat *en poste* in Dresden, Vienna and finally Paris. In 1773 he wrote that the house 'can never be made a tolerable habitation without immense expense which it can never deserve'. Nonetheless, a few years later he brought in the Edinburgh architect George Paterson to turn the palace into what Lord Stormont (who eventually succeeded to one of his famous uncle's Earldoms of Mansfield in 1793) called 'a very convenient habitation'.

It was not, though, until the time of his son, the 3rd Earl of Mansfield that Scone acquired its present Georgian Gothic appearance. 'Almost all people have follies', wrote this Lord Mansfield (a Fellow of the Royal Society and of the Society of Antiquaries), 'this is one which will have at least some advantage. The family had no residence and little interest any-

where. Though I shall have not ensured their interest yet I shall have given them a handsome and agreeable residence.'

In 1802, after toying with the idea of remodelling the interior in a post-Adam Classical style, the 3rd Earl commissioned the comparatively unknown William Atkinson, a pupil of James Wyatt, to construct a castellated affair in red sandstone. As the architectural historian Colin McWilliam has observed: 'Square, sober and reasonable, it has little to do with his later Abbotsford (see pages 186–195) and the romantic baronial style.'

The rooms are ample and well-lit, with Gothic details down to the pelmets and chandeliers. The halls and Gallery are attractively vaulted or beamed in a style that is suitably monastic in reference to Scone's sacred past. The costs of the lengthy building operations certainly confirmed the fears of Lord Mansfield's father about 'immense expense'. More than £60,000 had been spent by the end of 1811.

Whatever Atkinson's architecture may lack in excitement, it serves as a fine, understated setting for a marvellously varied collection of furniture and works of art – ranging from exotic 17th-century cabinets and tables from Germany and Italy to lacquered English Regency pieces and a feast of Boulle. The present arrangement of the interior owes much to the 7th Earl of Mansfield and his Countess, who courageously moved back into the Palace in the 1950s after it had been unoccupied – other than as a girls' school during the Second World War – for 30 years, and also to their son, the present Earl, and his Countess.

Lady Mansfield, a former chairman of the Scottish branch of the Historic Houses Association, has enthusiastically developed the opening arrangements of the Palace and is a knowledgeable custodian of its treasures. Lord Mansfield, a former Minister of State in both the Scottish and Northern Ireland Offices and latterly first Crown Estates Commissioner, takes a special interest in the 25,000-acre estate.

Indeed, Scone was one of the first historic houses open to the public to have a room exhibiting the workings of the estate, that vital support. A special corner of the policies, not far from the Palace and the Abbey ruins, is the Pinetum, dominated by a vast fir. Its original seed was sent back to Scotland in 1826 by a son of Scone, the celebrated horticulturist David Douglas, who began life as an under-gardener at the Palace.

His tragic end also had faint echoes of Scone – bearing in mind the trap-door banquet that undid the Picts. On one of his horticultural expeditions he fell into a pit dug by natives to catch wild bison. Unfortunately, he thereby found himself keeping close company with another occupant of the pit, a bull bison who in a most unneighbourly manner gored him to death.

LEFT
The State Bed in the Ambassador's Room. The ambassador, the 2nd Earl of Mansfield, had this regal bed made out of a canopy of State which was his perquisite as King George III's Ambassador to France in the 1770s. The King's arms and cypher are liberally displayed.

DALMENY HOUSE

WEST LOTHIAN

IN THE HALL at Dalmeny – the first Gothic Revival house in Scotland – hangs a striking conversation piece by Carlos Sancha of the present Earl of Rosebery and his family in the sweeping parkland beside the Firth of Forth. Painted in 1978, it depicts Lady Rosebery, a former stage designer whose imaginative flair has revitalized the interior of the house, holding some of the catalogues for the celebrated Mentmore Towers sale of the previous year – a permanent reminder of the event that effectively sparked off the present 'heritage industry'.

What was not generally appreciated at the time was that Lord and Lady Rosebery, far from selling up the entire treasures at Mentmore Towers in Buckinghamshire – which came into the family through the marriage in 1878 of the 5th Earl, the Prime Minister, to Hannah, only daughter and heiress of Baron Meyer de Rothschild – were merely rationalizing and concentrating their collections. Following the death of the 6th Earl of Rosebery, a legendary figure on the Turf, in 1974, the new Earl and his wife intended to offer Mentmore and most of its contents to the Government, but when that initiative famously floundered it was resolved to take the best things up to Scotland and to sell the rest which was unsuitable for Dalmeny. And so the cream of Baron Meyer's collection of 18th-century decorative arts – tapestries, carpets, porcelain, paintings and furniture – came north. The result is that this great house only a few miles from the centre of Edinburgh houses fabulous objects of a quality quite unsurpassed in Scotland.

The Dalmeny estate has been in the family since 1662 when Sir Archibald Primrose, a lawyer who had succeeded his father as Clerk to the Privy Council and eventually became Lord Clerk Register of Scotland, bought

the Barony of Barnbougle from the Hamiltons, Earls of Haddington. The original structure on the property, Barnbougle Castle, a 13th-century tower-house on the shore of the Firth of Forth, proved increasingly inconvenient as the sea battered away at the ancient walls. When questions were asked by the offspring of the 3rd Earl of Rosebery about when they might have a more up-to-date home, Lord Rosebery was wont to reply – even though he had been drenched by a wave that came in through the dining-room window – 'What was good enough for my grandfather should be good enough for my grandchildren.'

However, the 4th Earl of Rosebery, a member of the Society of Dilettanti, determined to build a completely new house on a separate site a quarter of a mile away. Before his father's death in 1814 he toyed with Classical designs by William Atkinson (who remodelled Scone Palace – see pages 72–81) and William Burn, but his careful observations in England and Wales – the Napoleonic Wars had precluded a Grand Tour – had converted his taste to Tudor Gothic.

Two architects, Jeffry Wyatt (later 'Wyatville' of Windsor Castle fame) and William Wilkins (best known for the National Gallery in London), were invited to submit designs for the new Dalmeny House. Wyatt sketched a Tudor Gothic pile, Wilkins a neo-Classical affair facing inland – away from the sea view. It seems, though, that Lord Rosebery was prejudiced in favour of Wilkins, an old Cambridge friend and fellow Dilettante, for he showed him Wyatt's design.

In any event, Wyatt was paid off and Wilkins duly produced a building which strongly recalled his and his client's East Anglian connections. Indeed the entrance front of Dalmeny is basically cribbed from the splendidly robust East Barsham Manor, which was built for Sir Henry Fermor in about 1520. The sea façade is more symmetrical with its central tower, octagonal turrets and regular mullion and transom windows. Inside, the principal rooms are Regency in style, but the mood of the Hall (with its hammer-beam ceiling), fan-vaulted corridor and Flemish stained-glass windows in the Gallery is romantically Gothic.

In 1819, two years after its completion, J.P. Neale described the new Dalmeny House in his *Views of the Seats of Noblemen and Gentlemen* as being 'calculated more for comfort and convenience than for show'. Twenty-five years later, when the young Queen Victoria visited her former bridesmaid, Lady Dalmeny (whose husband was not to succeed to the Earldom of Rosebery as, having advocated exercise as a means to healthy living for the middle classes, he expired from pleurisy brought on by a midwinter walk back from Edinburgh's Turkish baths), she was full of praise for the comfort – and the sea view. The present Roseberys find that

Wilkins's sensible adaptation of the historical style to contemporary life has enabled them to live in 'comfort and convenience' upstairs (thereby enjoying a better view of the sea) while the rest of the house has worked remarkably well for 'show'.

Today, thanks to Lady Rosebery's dramatic eye, it is undoubtedly some show. The contents have to be seen to be believed. Apart from the exquisite French 18th-century furniture, tapestries, Sèvres porcelain and paintings from Mentmore in the Drawing Room, there are early Scottish portraits of the Primroses, 17th-century Scottish furniture, Burns mementoes, Goya tapestries and, in the Dining Room, a majestic group of masterpieces by Reynolds, Gainsborough, Raeburn and Lawrence. The former billiard room is devoted to the unrivalled Napoleonic collection formed by the 5th Earl of Rosebery.

ABOVE
The Dining Room, hung with portraits from the collection of the 5th Earl of Rosebery, the late-Victorian Prime Minister. On the far wall, to the left, is the 3rd Earl, portrayed by Sir Henry Raeburn in Thistle robes and one of his three wigs of varying lengths. To the right is Admiral Lord Rodney by Thomas Gainsborough.

The story goes that the 5th Earl, as a boy at Eton, expressed the triple ambition – gloriously fulfilled – of becoming Prime Minister, winning the Derby and marrying a Rothschild. He collected objects and paintings not solely for their artistic merit but because of their connection with people he considered historically important; the Napoleonic accumulation at Dalmeny is the largest of these 'associative collections'.

Besides adorning the main house with cherished objects, the 5th Earl also rebuilt, in 1881, Barnbougle Castle, which had previously been left to the sea birds. The old place was partly demolished when explosives, stowed

BELOW
Joseph Nollekens's marble bust of the 2nd Marquess of Rockingham in the Dining Room at Dalmeny. One of Lord Rosebery's predecessors as Prime Minister, the Whiggish Lord Rockingham, infuriated King George III by his support for American independence.

RIGHT
The vaulted Gothic corridor which gives access to the State rooms.

for quarrying, were accidentally ignited. Dalmeny itself suffered a serious fire during the Second World War after which the 6th Earl of Rosebery and his Countess brought in the architect 'Paul' Geddes Hyslop to carry out a sensitive restoration. Hyslop gave the Library a deeply coved ceiling, reused Wilkins's oak bookcases (salvaged from the flames) and installed a mid-18th-century Rococo chimneypiece (from the demolished Rosebery town house in Berkeley Square) to create a delightfully comfortable ensemble. It was also in the aftermath of the Second World War that Dalmeny earned the right to be considered the birthplace of the Edinburgh Festival – thanks to the enterprise of the 6th Earl, chairman of the newly formed Scottish Tourist Board, and of his Countess, Eva, an accomplished amateur pianist.

If a visitor is, understandably, quite overwhelmed by the sensational art-historical experience on offer in this treasure-house, he can turn with relief to the leathery masculine comfort of the 6th Earl's sitting-room – a

BELOW
The 6th Earl of Rosebery's snug sitting room, well-stocked with masculine comfort and sporting memorabilia. Over the fireplace is a painting by Alexander Nasmyth of the 3rd Earl and his family outside Barnbougle Castle in 1784.

The entrance front: Tudor Perpendicular comes to Scotland by way of East Anglia (the architect William Wilkins copied much of the detail from East Barsham Manor in Norfolk). The equine statue is by Ernst Boehm of 'King Tom' (1873), the foundation stallion of Baron Meyer de Rothschild's stud. It was moved here from Mentmore in 1982.

richly atmospheric sportsman's 'den' redolent of the Turf, the chase and the cricket field. The Rosebery racing colours (rose and primrose) together with the gold, red and black of I Zingari and the chocolate of Surrey conjure up 'great days in the distance enchanted'. In his younger days, as Lord Dalmeny, the 6th Earl captained Surrey at cricket and awarded Jack Hobbs his county cap at The Oval.

The sporting colours chime with the present Countess's view of life in great houses. 'Everybody lives in, and enjoys, their own "fruit salad"', says Lady Rosebery, who opens Dalmeny to the public in the early part of the week during July and August, and for corporate entertaining. 'But the trouble with a "stately home" is that the bowl is too big. Each generation has to sell a few good pieces, buy some of what they personally like, and push the mother-in-law's favourites to the back. We've had to distill it, and put it into different subject areas, so it is easier to understand and enjoy.' No 'fruit salad', though, could be more sympathetically arranged or contain so many wonderfully exotic ingredients as Dalmeny.

KINROSS HOUSE

KINROSS-SHIRE

IN A TOUR of Scotland in 1722 Daniel Defoe, celebrated as the author of *Robinson Crusoe*, found, at the west end of Loch Leven, 'the most beautiful and regular piece of Architecture (for a private Gentleman's Seat) in all Scotland, perhaps in Great Britain.' As Defoe noted, this 'noble palace' of Kinross House had been built by 'that great architect Sir William Bruce' on an estate bought in the 'reign of King Charles II' from the Douglases, Earls of Morton. 'The House', Defoe enthused, 'is a picture, 'tis all Beauty, the Stone is white (and fine), the Order regular, the Contrivance elegant, the Workmanship exquisite.'

A visitor today – and it should be noted that only the gardens of Kinross House are opened regularly to the public by the present owner, Mr James Montgomery, heir of Sir David Montgomery, Bt – can do little more than echo Defoe's sentiments. For, as Sir David points out, the remarkable thing is that, during the 300 years since it was built, Kinross has not been structurally altered or significantly changed in any way. What you see is an authentic example not only of late 17th-century architecture but also of landscaping; as Defoe said, 'the great avenue from the town of Kinross is the noblest you can imagine'.

The vista does not end with the Classical symmetry of the house; it carries on through to the formal garden (magnificently re-created by Sir Basil Montgomery, 5th Bt, at the beginning of the 20th century) and thence to Loch Leven itself. Bruce ingeniously planned the axis of his house and garden to focus on a prospect of Lochleven Castle – through the delightful 'Fish Gate', with its cherubs and cornucopia dipping down to a basket of wriggling fish, representing the 11 species caught (at that time) in the loch.

PRECEDING PAGES
The main staircase carved
from oak by (in all
probability) the Dutch
craftsman Jan van sant
Voort, who worked with
Sir William Bruce at
Edinburgh's royal palace
of Holyroodhouse.

LEFT
View to Loch Leven
Castle from the formal
gardens through the Fish
Gates.

The castle was an ancient stronghold of the Douglas family and is known to history as the prison of Mary Queen of Scots from the summer of 1567 to the spring of 1568. Her gaoler, Sir William Douglas (later 5th Earl of Morton), had been implicated in the murder of Mary's favourite, the musician David Rizzio, but Sir William's younger son, George, gallantly helped the Queen to escape by boat across the loch.

In the 17th century the Douglases, Earls of Morton, were staunch supporters of King Charles I and paid dearly for their over-generous contributions to the Royalist cause. By 1675 the 8th Earl of Morton was in such straitened circumstances that he had to sell his Kinross-shire estate to Sir William Bruce, Bt, a prosperous courtier who had played a significant role in the Restoration of King Charles II. Bruce had begun life with no great fortune, but was well connected and had a keen eye for opportunity. His moment came when he acted as the go-between during the negotiations by General Monk, the Parliamentary Commonwealth's representative in Scotland, and the exiled King Charles in Holland. Once the Restoration came Bruce was showered with profitable offices. As a passionate amateur of architecture and gardening, the office that would have given Bruce most satisfaction was his appointment, in 1671, as 'surveyor, contriver and overseer of all the works at the palace of Holyroodhouse, and of such other castles and palaces in Scotland as the King shall appoint to be repaired.'

Apart from Holyroodhouse, which he virtually rebuilt, Bruce's architectural talents also flourished at Thirlestane and Hopetoun (see pages 64–71; 106–15), but Kinross is his master work – not least because it has remained largely untouched. A pioneer of Palladianism in Scotland, Bruce has been hailed as Caledonia's answer to Inigo Jones and Sir Christopher Wren. Yet while Kinross fully deserves the reputation of being Scotland's first great Classical country house, what gives the place its extraordinary charm is the hint of Scottish vernacular here and there – particularly in the Stables.

The main house appears to have been built largely between 1685 and 1691. The Cleish stone, which gives Kinross its special character, is not so much 'white', as Defoe described it, as a warm yellow streaked with reddish-brown veins. The stone is laid in massive blocks, giving the house an impressive solidity, and adorned with Corinthian pilasters and carvings round the central doors and windows.

An account of June 1686 records that two Dutch stone-carvers, 'Peeter Paull Boyse & Cornelius Vanerba' were paid £12 10s, though the actual signature of the receipt is by one 'Cornillis van nerven'. It is thought that the Dutchmen were mainly employed on the garlanded cartouches above

BELOW
The west (entrance) front
from the avenue.

the pavilion doors, the lion masks on the curving screen walls and, quite possibly, the endearing embellishments of the Fish Gate.

By this stage, the stables had been roofed but the main block had only risen as high as the basement. The summer of 1686 also marked a turning point in Sir William Bruce's career. The new Catholic King, James VII of Scotland and II of England, with whom the staunchly Episcopalian Bruce had never hit it off, sacked his brother's faithful courtier from the Privy Council.

Although the entrance floor rooms were finished off much as Bruce originally intended, the *piano nobile*, or grand suite of rooms, on the first floor, remained undecorated. Indeed the present coved plaster ceiling which presides over Bruce's splendid double-height 'Great Sallon' was not inserted until the beginning of the 20th century.

In 1775, some 50 years after Defoe's rapturous observations, Sylas Neville visited Kinross and found it 'from the negligence and indifferent

ABOVE
The Ballroom, Sir William Bruce's 'Great Sallon', which occupies most of the first floor at Kinross. Sir Basil Montgomery, 5th Bt, added the coved ceiling in the early 20th century

RIGHT
The Drawing Room, or as Sir William Bruce called it, the Garden Hall. The overdoor paintings were supplied by Alexander Brand of Edinburgh in 1692.

circumstances of the owner [James Bruce Carstairs]... much out of repair.' Neville concluded, 'A rich Nabob might make something very magnificent here'. Sure enough, it was a Nabob, though not a very rich one, who bought Kinross a couple of years later in the person of George Graham, a merchant of Calcutta.

In 1819 Graham's son, Thomas, died, leaving two daughters and a situation slightly reminiscent of the more or less contemporaneous scramble among the Royal Dukes to produce an heir to the throne. The Kinross estate, decreed Thomas Graham, was to be inherited by whichever of his daughters had a son who first reached 21. As the genial Sir David Montgomery relates, 'The Montgomery of the day got off the mark like a shot and married Helen Graham [Thomas's younger daughter], who gave birth to a boy six months before her less pretty sister – which, I might add, is the only reason we're here today'.

Yet, while continuing to maintain the Kinross estate, the Montgomerys preferred to live at their ancestral home of Stobo Castle in Peeblesshire. So Kinross House slept, mercifully unspoilt, through the rest of the 19th century.

Then, in 1902, the baronetcy and the estates passed to Basil Montgomery, whose love of architecture and gardening hardly fell short of Sir William Bruce's own. Determined to awake the Sleeping Beauty, Sir Basil moved into Kinross and set about restoring Bruce's masterpiece to its full glory. The main house was sensitively repaired, with Sir Basil himself being responsible for the new ceiling in the Ballroom. He took the plasterwork over the great staircase as his model and, as Sir David comments, 'he didn't do a bad job'. Many of the family portraits were brought back (including Bruce's own) and the rooms were filled with fine furniture.

Above all, Sir Basil remade the glorious formal garden – with, as the memorial plaque in one of the pavilions at Kinross phrases it, 'timeless devotion, unerring judgment and with joy'. Today it ranks as one of the finest formal gardens in Scotland and is regularly open to the public.

LEFT
Lady Montgomery, the former Helen Graham and heiress of Kinross, by Sir Henry Raeburn in the Ballroom.

RIGHT
Atlas in the gardens – a statue brought to Kinross in the early 1900s by Sir Basil Montgomery, 5th Bt.

NEWHAILES

EAST LOTHIAN

WE WERE fortunate to visit Newhailes, an almost incredible survival of the Scottish Enlightenment now surrounded by the suburban sprawl of Musselburgh on the outskirts of Edinburgh, at a crucial moment in its history. For, in January 1997, the last private owner, Lady Antonia Dalrymple, widow of Sir Mark Dalrymple, 3rd (and last) Bt of Newhailes, was preparing to move out as the house was about to be formally handed over into the care of the National Trust for Scotland after a remarkable rescue act to save this exquisite ensemble from being dispersed.

Since Sir Mark's death in 1971, Lady Antonia had fought valiantly to preserve this 'Time Capsule' in its increasingly unpromising setting, but the maintenance costs had become impossibly high. Grasping the singular importance of a place nicely described by one of its new National Trust champions as 'a battered old jewelbox, dusty and much the worse for wear – inside, to your surprise, are unique and priceless treasures', the Heritage lobby acted in unison to find the £12.7 million necessary for Newhailes' restoration and secure future. The Heritage Lottery Fund came up with £8 million; Historic Scotland granted £1.45 million for repairs; the National Art Collections Fund contributed £245,000 for the purchase of four of the outstanding portraits in the house (including two by Allan Ramsay); and the balance was to be sought through public appeal by the NTS.

We were lucky enough to glimpse Newhailes in its 'Before' state – decayed, intimate, idiosyncratic to a degree, magically untouched – while scholarly and sensitive preparations were already being laid by the NTS curatorial team for the long haul to 'After'. The photographer was privileged to capture it before the sea change.

PRECEDING PAGES
The Dining Room, painted by James
Norie in 1739 in 'olive oyl' and
bewitchingly unchanged.

ABOVE
The Winter Drawing Room, hung with
family portraits by Allan Ramsay and Sir
Henry Raeburn and boasting a richly
carved chimneypiece by Sir Henry
Cheere.

RIGHT
'The most learned room in Europe',
according to Dr Johnson: the Library
was once the epitome of the Scottish
Enlightenment of the 18th century but
is presently denuded of books. Now
that Newhailes has been rescued by the
nation and vested in the National Trust
for Scotland, it is hoped that the
National Library of Scotland will be
able to return Lord Hailes's great
collection.

The sea itself seems to play a significant part in the story of several great
Scottish houses. At Newhailes one is constantly reminded of the ocean
not only by its physical proximity – the vista over the Firth of Forth is mirac-
ulously retained with the monstrosities in between conveniently hidden
as if by a fortuitous 'ha-ha' – but by the plethora of shells that adorn
the interior. They are to be spotted in every conceivable place. And in
several instances they are not imitations but genuine seashells, gilded for
decoration. It is thought that this riot of shells may allude to the Rococo

style enthusiastically adopted at Newhailes by Sir James Dalrymple, 2nd Bt of Hailes, in the 1720s and 1730s.

Sir James's father, Sir David Dalrymple, 1st Bt of Hailes, Auditor of the Exchequer, had acquired the property, previously called Whitehill, in 1707 – the year of the Act of Union with England, for which he was a commissioner. At that stage it was actually called Broughton House, for five years earlier the 2nd Lord Bellenden of Broughton, no Croesus himself, had picked it up from its bankrupt builder, James Smith. The wretched architect's financial plight can be explained by the fact that he and his wife had no less than two dozen children.

As built by him in about 1686, the seven-bay Whitehill would hardly have been big enough to accommodate Smith's ever-expanding brood. Nonetheless, the design of his pioneering Palladian villa is a fascinating precursor of the celebrated palaces he went on to build: Hamilton (the ducal

ABOVE LEFT
The portrait by Sir John Medina in the elaborate overmantel of 1742 shows Lord Hailes's father and grandfather, the 1st and 2nd Dalrymple Baronets. Sir David, the 1st Bt, began the Library; Sir James, the 2nd Bt, completed its progress into a great room.

ABOVE RIGHT
The gorgeously cluttered China Closet.

seat demolished in the 1920s) and Dalkeith (a property of the Dukes of Buccleuch now let out to an American university).

The shell of Smith's late 17th-century Whitehill survives, together with his twisting spiral staircase and the wainscoting in the Chinese Room. What we see at Newhailes today, though, is predominantly the result of the Dalrymples' radical remodelling and redecoration of the 18th century.

Like so many great Scots families, the Dalrymples' fortunes were founded in the Law. Sir David Dalrymple, Newhailes' new owner, was a younger son of the 1st Viscount of Stair, President of the Court of Session, and his elder brother, John (later 1st Earl of Stair), made his name as Lord Justice Clerk – before earning notoriety as the Joint Secretary of State who authorized the treacherous massacre of the Clan Macdonald at Glencoe in 1692.

Whatever the malignance of Lord Stair, though, there was nothing cursed about Newhailes. Far from being a haunt of evil, it became the epitome of the 18th-century Enlightenment, with a Library memorably described by Dr Samuel Johnson as 'the most learned room in Europe'.

The Library wing was begun by Sir David Dalrymple shortly before his death in 1721. His dream of enlarging Newhailes was realized with consummate style by his son and successor, Sir James. A pretty new entrance hall was created which was adorned with plasterwork by Thomas Clayton, complete with ornate swags, flowers, birds, trophies and lions' manes fluttering in the Forth breeze. The Dining Room extension was ingeniously disguised by a screen of two pairs of Ionic columns.

The most remarkable interiors of all come in the east wing. First, of course, the Library, which was enriched by Sir James with a splendid new marble chimneypiece (unattributed, though the great Sir Henry Cheere provided three others in the house) and a plaster overmantel by Clayton framing Sir John Medina's double-portrait of Sir James as a boy with his father. The Library enjoyed its zenith in the time of Sir James's own son, another Sir David, better known by his Session title of Lord Hailes, who wrote *The Annals of Scotland* on the mahogany writing table here.

It is a measure of Newhailes' extraordinary spirit that this noble room still had a potent atmosphere even though the towering shelves had been emptied of books. The collection was accepted by the Treasury in lieu of tax on the late Sir Mark Dalrymple's estate in the 1970s and placed in the National Library of Scotland. The likely return of the volumes to the shelves in due course is one of the most exciting prospects offered by Newhailes' reincarnation as a National Trust for Scotland showplace.

The showing of the China Closet off the Library will present particular logistical problems for the Trust. This astonishing arrangement, as well

ABOVE
The entrance front, framed by Palladian gatepiers. To the original seven-bay villa of the late 1680s was added, to the right, the Library wing of 1719–20 and, to the left, the wing containing the 'Great Apartment' of rooms, completed in 1733. The plate-glass windows were an unsympathetic Victorian addition (and it is hoped that they will be replaced).

LEFT
View through doorway of the Entrance Hall, which contains some of Thomas Clayton's best plasterwork (of 1742).

as the alterations to Norie's panels in the Chinese Room, and much else besides, belong to the hitherto underrated contribution made to Newhailes during the 19th century.

Students of country-house life will wait with interest to see what the NTS can uncover about this period. Lord Hailes's redoubtable spinster daughter, Christian Dalrymple, a staunch philanthropist and friend to the local miners' wives, ruled at Newhailes for nearly 50 years. When a young man had the impertinence to ask the hunchbacked old lady why she had never married, Miss Dalrymple modestly responded, 'Much to the credit of mankind, no one has ever asked me'.

Christian's nephew and successor, Sir Charles Dalrymple Fergusson, 5th Bt of Kilkerran, called in William Burn to make various improvements in 1839, a year after his aunt's death. Further changes were made later in the 19th century by his younger son, Charles, who took the name of Dalrymple and was given a new Baronetcy (his elder brother succeeded to Kilkerran and the Fergusson title). Some of these were unfortunate, especially the substitution of plate-glass for a few of the Classical sash windows. Replacing the proper fenestration will help to rejuvenate the previously dilapidated facade and should rank high in the National Trust for Scotland's heroic crusade to preserve the magic of Newhailes for posterity.

HOPETOUN HOUSE

WEST LOTHIAN

IF PUT on the spot and asked to single out a 'Great House' in Scotland, one would have to choose Hopetoun, the largest and most sensational country house of its kind in the country. With its vast forecourt and sweeping, curved colonnades, this Baroque palace of the Hope family, Earls of Hopetoun and latterly Marquesses of Linlithgow, has understandably been called 'the Scottish Versailles'.

Not the least of Hopetoun's thrills is its proximity to the Firth of Forth. The sea could be said to have played a crucial part in the history of Hopetoun. The family tradition goes that in 1682 John Hope of Hopetoun – who four years earlier had bought the estate on which the present house stands from the Setons – lost his life in a shipwreck through giving up his seat in a lifeboat to the Duke of York (later King James VII of Scotland and II of England). According to one account of the sinking of the frigate *Gloucester*, the Duke's dogs were also saved but poor Hope and several other gallant Scots gentlemen who were in attendance perished.

By way of compensation, as it were, Queen Anne created John Hope of Hopetoun's son and successor, Charles, Earl of Hopetoun when he came of age in 1703. The fortunes of the Hope family – a respectable dynasty of Edinburgh merchants, lawyers and courtiers – had been handsomely consolidated by John's father, Sir James Hope, an expert mineralogist who skilfully exploited the lead mines inherited by his wife, Anne Foulis, in Lanarkshire.

After John Hope had drowned, the development of his new estate at Hopetoun was left in the capable hands of his widow, Lady Margaret, eldest daughter of the 4th Earl of Haddington. The architect chosen was Sir William Bruce, the Palladian pioneer and hero of the chapter on Kin-

PREDEDING PAGES
Sir William Bruce's pine-panelled staircase with elaborate carvings by Alexander
Eizart, who worked with the Architect Royal at Holyroodhouse. The hand-rail and
banisters are of oak. The neo-Classical murals are modern, being painted in 1967
by the Scottish *trompe l'oeil* artist William McLaren as a memorial to the first
Marchioness of the 3rd Marquess, the former Vivien Kenyon-Slaney from Hatton
Grange, Shropshire, who died in 1963. They reflect Lady Linlithgow's love of
Hopetoun and its variety of wildlife.

ABOVE
Detail of William Adam's
east front, showing steps
and colonnade.

RIGHT
Enfilade through State
rooms.

ross House (see pages 90–7). From 1699 onwards he built a restrained, urbane gentleman's seat in the Classical manner. This would surely have earned him an even greater claim to posterity had not Lady Margaret's son Charles – under the influence of his flamboyant brother-in-law, the 2nd Marquess of Annandale – decided to make a bigger splash with the help of William Adam.

Today Hopetoun tends to be thought of as an Adam house – naturally enough, as it is not only one of William's chief works but also a significant staging-post for his son, the great Robert, whose courtyard pavilions and their remarkable towers are among his earliest independent commissions. From the front, it is Adam all the way – and very magnificent it is too. Yet, walk round to the back and you will see that Bruce's quiet voice, reticent and dignified, can still be heard, emanating from the perfectly proportioned west, or garden, front. In the eyes of many discerning architectural judges this side of Hopetoun is the more satisfactory of the two.

Inside the house, as well, the Adams did not carry everything before them. The panelled Garden Parlour, the Libraries and the Bruce Bedchamber (designed for the young 1st Earl of Hopetoun) all still evoke Sir William's exquisite late 17th-century taste, as does the main staircase, with its luscious carving by Alexander Eizart, who worked with Bruce, the 'Architect Royal', at the Palace of Holyroodhouse.

The seeds of the brevity of Bruce's house at Hopetoun were sown in the same year as he began building operations, for in 1699 the 17-year-old Charles Hope of Hopetoun married Lady Henrietta Johnston, only daughter of the 1st Marquess of Annandale. Lady Henrietta's precocious connoisseur brother, James, later the 2nd Marquess of Annandale, had strong views on architecture and urged his brother-in-law to think big. He himself had remodelled another Bruce house, at Craighall, Fife, to the designs of William Adam, an adventurous Classical architect inspired by the dramatic styles of Sir John Vanbrugh and James Gibbs. Adam – who is said to have been apprenticed to Bruce at Hopetoun as a boy in the early 1700s – made his name with the publication of his first volume of *Vitruvius Scoticus* in 1720.

The next year – in which Charles Hopetoun's bachelor brother-in-law also happened to succeed to the Marquessate of Annandale – William Adam began transforming Bruce's house at Hopetoun. Bruce had built a grand entrance forecourt but within a mere 20 years this was to be swept away for something even grander. First of all, Adam extended one wing; then, in 1725, he began the colonnades; and in 1727 came the plan for a completely new façade.

Yet when the 2nd Earl of Hopetoun inherited the property in 1742, William Adam's newly recast 'Great Apartment', the enfilade of State rooms

LEFT

The Yellow Drawing Room, originally the State Dining Room, with joinery by the Hopetoun estate craftsman John Paterson, stucco ceiling by John Dawson and furniture by James Cullen. The large painting on the left is *The Adoration of the Shepherds* (School of Rubens). The Scottish artist Henry Raeburn was knighted in this room by King George IV during his visit to Hopetoun in 1822.

running north from the entrance hall, was still an unfinished shell. The decoration and furnishing of these rooms was to extend over 26 years and to deploy the talents of William Adam's sons, Robert and John. They were responsible for the pretty Rococo coved ceilings in the Green Dining Room (now the Yellow Drawing Room) and the Red Drawing Room with plasterwork by John Dawson.

The 2nd Earl was so pleased with Robert Adam's work that in 1754 he suggested the young architect should accompany his brother Charles on an Italian tour and share expenses. This celebrated trip was to have far-reaching effects on the course of architecture in Britain. Its immediate consequence at Hopetoun was the great marble chimneypiece in the Red Drawing Room, the design of which was sent by Robert Adam from Rome.

The final room in the Great Apartment, the State Dining Room, was created early in the 19th century by combining the old Ante-Chamber and Great Bedchamber. This was done for General the 4th Earl of Hopetoun, a Peninsular War commander, to the designs of the architect James Gillespie Graham. The General, who also added greatly to Hopetoun's

RIGHT

The Bruce Bedchamber, originally part of a suite designed by Sir William Bruce for the young Charles Hope, later 1st Earl of Hopetoun. The gilded wall paintings (of 1791–2) are by James Norie, the Edinburgh decorator, who also worked at Newhailes (see pages 98–105). The State Bed was supplied in 1768 by Mathias Lock of London for the Great Bedchamber.

collection of Old Master paintings, entertained King George IV on his famous visit to Edinburgh in 1822. The King, no mean builder himself, was suitably impressed by Hopetoun – 'By Gad, you've got big pleasures', he observed of Adam's landscaped 'policies' – even if he lunched only modestly off turtle soup and three glasses of wine.

Subsequent Earls of Hopetoun continued to improve their estates and then, in the late 19th and early 20th centuries, the family became prominent in international affairs when the 7th Earl, later the 1st Marquess of

LEFT
The State Dining Room, created in the early
19th century by, in all probability, James
Gillespie Graham, who combined the old
Ante-Chamber and Great Bedchamber. The
original doors and architraves of the earlier
rooms were reused as part of a lavish Regency
ensemble, complete with gilt wallpaper and a
gilded cornice and sunburst ceiling rose.

BELOW
View of the Forth road and rail
bridges from Hopetoun's roof.

Linlithgow, served as the first Governor-General of the Commonwealth
of Australia and the 2nd Marquess of Linlithgow as Viceroy and Governor-General of India. Full-length portraits of these pro-consular figures
dominate the coolly Palladian Entrance Hall at Hopetoun and their
Imperial experiences add lustre to the mementoes in the Family Museum.

The 3rd Marquess of Linlithgow was taken prisoner at Dunkirk in
1940 with the 51st Highland Division and ended up in the Nazi fortress
of Colditz as one of the '*Prominente*'. In 1974 he and his son, the Earl of
Hopetoun (now the 4th Marquess), were instrumental in setting up an
independent charitable trust to preserve Hopetoun House with its historic contents and surrounding landscape for the benefit of the public.
The Preservation Trust has done much good work in educating the young
to appreciate Hopetoun's heritage.

MELLERSTAIN

BERWICKSHIRE

AT THIS stage of the narrative we have emphatically arrived in the Age of Adam. Mellerstain – an enchanting 18th-century 'toy fort' in the Borders which many architectural enthusiasts regard as their favourite great house in Scotland – is an especially instructive example for it allows us to contrast the architectural styles of Father and Son, William and Robert.

Mellerstain was built in two distinct stages: first came the wings in 1725 from William Adam and then, curiously, some half-a-century later, the large central block by Robert. As one enters the spacious forecourt the difference is apparent enough, with the projection in the centre being a typically bold flourish of the younger Adam. By contrast, the south façade at the back, looking out over the Edwardian formal gardens to the Cheviots, is flatter and more subtle.

For all its jolly castellated skyline and the warmth of its local yellowish stone, Mellerstain strikes some visitors as a little severe. Inside, though, Robert Adam really let rip. The results can hardly fail to inspire the most curmudgeonly critic. The ceilings, friezes and fireplaces sing with a refreshingly cool, Classical assurance.

There can be no lovelier interior in Scotland than the Library at Mellerstain with its Adam bookcases and green-and-white marble chimneypiece. The gaily coloured ceiling of 1770, adorned by Zucci, is rightly considered one of Robert Adam's masterpieces. Another splendid ceiling, dated three years later and decorated with eagles and sphinxes, is to be found at the centre of the garden enfilade in the Music Room, which Robert Adam originally designed as a dining room.

The family portraits in this room of Baillies, Humes and Hamiltons help bring Mellerstain's genealogy to life. The Baillie family acquired the

estate in 1642 when George Baillie, son of a prosperous Edinburgh merchant, was granted a Royal Charter. The old house here, known as Whiteside,
seems to have stood not far from the present site – indeed it may well
have survived for a while as a ruin between William Adam's two new wings,
which may account for the time-lapse of nearly 50 years before the main
block was built.

During the religious troubles of the 17th century the Baillies were
staunch Covenanters and in 1676 Robert Baillie, George's son and successor, was imprisoned for rescuing his brother-in-law from what he thought
to be illegal arrest. As Robert languished in the Tolbooth in Edinburgh,
he was visited in jail by the plucky Grisell Hume, 12-year-old daughter of
his political ally and local MP, Sir Patrick Hume, 2nd Bt. Sir Patrick had
entrusted a secret message to this determined young go-between who
was to play a leading role in the saga of Mellerstain. The romantic story goes
that young Grisell met her future husband, George Baillie, Robert's son,
while he happened to be visiting his father in the Tolbooth at the same time
as her own brave mission.

PRECEDING PAGES
View of the garden front
from across the lake.
This was enlarged by Sir
Reginald Blomfield and
linked to the terraces in
1909.

BELOW
Robert Adam's
beautifully proportioned
Front Hall, with one of
its apsidal ends.

ABOVE LEFT
A corner of the Drawing Room, showing Allan Ramsay's portrait of Rachel Hamilton and her brother Charles, 1740. They were children of Lord Binning and his wife, Rachel Baillie, the ultimate heiress of Mellerstain.

ABOVE RIGHT
Enfilade through the State rooms.

Many vicissitudes had to be endured before they could marry and settle at Mellerstain. In 1684 Robert Baillie was executed for high treason and the Mellerstain estate was forfeited. The Hume estate of Polwarth suffered a similar fate the next year when Sir Patrick himself was fortunate not to end with his head on the block for his part in the Monmouth Rebellion.

In any event, the Humes took off for Holland where they were joined by Grisell's young friend George Baillie. Times were hard, and owing to the poor health of her mother, the burden of managing the impoverished refugee household fell upon Grisell, the eldest girl of no less than 18 children. Her housekeeping skills were to form the basis for her *Household Book*, which was eventually published and hailed as a classic of Scottish social history.

Grisell and George were finally married in 1691 by which time the Hume and Baillie estates had been restored. George Baillie of Mellerstain went on to become an MP and one of the architects of the Act of Union

in 1707. For the architecture of a new house in keeping with his status, he and Lady Grisell (as she became styled when her father was elevated to the Earldom of Marchmont in 1697) turned to William Adam, fresh down from his triumphs at Hopetoun (see pages 106–15) and already established as Scotland's leading Classical architect. Adam drew up plans for a Palladian centre-piece (never built) with two wings. The foundation stone of the east wing, was laid in September 1725.

The original scheme provided for the two wings to be connected by corridors, but as built there was nothing between them – except perhaps the ruins of old Whiteside. The two wings were, though, fine houses in themselves and survive as interesting examples of Scottish architecture of an earlier epoch.

It is pleasant to imagine Lady Grisell and her family living contentedly here in the 1720s after all the traumas of the past. By all accounts she and George were a devoted couple. 'They never had the shadow of a quarrel

ABOVE
The Library: one of Robert Adam's outstanding creations, with an exquisite decorated ceiling in the original colours of 1773. The circular oil painting of Minerva is by Zucci. The high-backed chair in the foreground is William and Mary period, *circa* 1700.

RIGHT
The main staircase, which rises in two flights and proceeds in one.

or misunderstanding or dryness betwixt them, not for a moment', recalled their elder daughter, Lady Murray. 'He never went abroad but she went to the window to look after him, and so she did that very day he fell ill the last time he went abroad, never taking her eyes from him as long as he was in sight.'

George Baillie died in 1738, to be followed eight years later by Lady Grisell. Mellerstain eventually passed to their grandson, George Hamilton, second son of their younger daughter, Rachel, who married Lord Binning, heir of the 6th Earl of Haddington. The Hamiltons, Earls of Haddington, had been one of the most prosperous dynasties in Scotland since the

BELOW LEFT
Detail of garden statuary.

BELOW RIGHT
The entrance front: the central block is by Robert Adam, the wings by his father, William.

early 17th century when Sir Thomas Hamilton, an eminent lawyer, developed the mines on his estates and acquired extensive Abbey lands, such as Tyninghame.

Rachel's younger son, George Baillie (who changed his name from Hamilton) of Mellerstain was a man of taste, having done the Grand Tour, and naturally turned to William Adam's fashionable son, Robert, to complete the house his grandparents had started in 1725. It is clear from the plans, copiously initialled 'G.B.', that Baillie did not give Robert Adam a completely free hand. Here was a client who knew his own mind: he did not want a vast palace but a comfortable country house on a human scale, with just a hint of the castle on the exterior to reflect the swing away from the purely Classical.

Consequently, the creative discipline imposed on Adam produced an exquisite gem in miniature. The intimacy of the atmosphere at Mellerstain could be said to be a happy tribute to the creative conflict between George Baillie and Robert Adam. Much as one sympathizes with Baillie, though, and admires his control over Adam, it can only be a matter for regret that the lustrous design for the ceiling of the Great Gallery was never carried out. The barrel vault of this magnificent room – a wonderful surprise at the top of the house – cries out for Robert Adam's finishing touches. Nonetheless, there is still plenty of delicious detail to enjoy at Mellerstain which has remained joyfully unchanged since Adam completed work here in about 1778.

In 1858 George Baillie's grandson and namesake succeeded his second cousin, the 9th Earl of Haddington, in the Earldom and assumed the surname of Baillie-Hamilton. Mellerstain's next owner, the 11th Earl of Haddington, a prominent freemason and agriculturalist, brought in the Edwardian architect Sir Reginald Blomfield in 1909 to transform the vista from the garden front. The slope which fell from the south front of the house to the lake at the foot of the hill was ingeniously adapted into a series of garden terraces. Blomfield altered and enlarged the lake so as to link it to the terraces with a glorious sweep of lawn. The result is a noble composition – seemingly reaching, as the present Earl of Haddington nicely observes, 'to infinity'.

Lord Haddington, a professional photographer celebrated for his work recording the mysterious rashes of crop circles, has a keen eye for beauty and he and his wife, Jane, have done much to enhance the friendly spirit of Mellerstain. They and their young family live in the west wing, which was converted from its former use as a stable block by the architect Schomberg Scott in 1975. In 1986, Lord Haddington established a charitable trust to secure the future of this lovable place for posterity.

ARNISTON HOUSE

MIDLOTHIAN

ARNISTON, set in a fine park beneath the Moorfoot Hills and yet only 11 miles south of Edinburgh, deserves to be much better known. With the spirited efforts of its present châtelaine, Althea Dundas Bekker to restore the house after savage outbreaks of dry rot, and the fact that it is now open to the public in the summer months, it surely will be. For it is a splendid example of William Adam's work: a handsome Palladian structure flanked by two wings and containing a breathtaking Baroque hall which automatically puts Arniston in the 'great' class of Scottish country houses.

Adam arrived at Arniston in 1725 after making his mark as a mason at another Midlothian seat, Mavisbank (now a ruin), under the patronage of Sir John Clerk of Penicuik, a noted champion of Palladianism. Clerk took his protégé to see Sir John Vanbrugh's theatrical flourishes at Castle Howard and elsewhere, which greatly excited Adam.

Whereas Sir John Clerk of Penicuik knew precisely what he wanted and kept Adam's new enthusiasms under rigorous control, his next clients, the Dundases of Arniston, a Presbyterian legal dynasty, did not aspire to be arbiters of taste and gave their architect a much freer hand. Nonetheless, Adam was constrained by the Dundas family's desire for the new seat at Arniston to incorporate at least part of the existing, early 17th-century towerhouse on the site.

The Dundases had acquired the estate in 1571 at the insistence of the second wife of George Dundas, 16th Laird of Dundas (the ancient seat of the family near Queensferry, West Lothian), Katherine Oliphant, who planned for her son, James, to be comfortably set up with a property of his own. James Dundas duly established himself at Arniston, built an open courtyard house, carried out agricultural improvements and founded

a dynasty that achieved almost as much distinction in the Law as the Adam family was to achieve in architecture. Indeed no less than five successive Lairds of Arniston rose to the bench of the Supreme Court of Scotland – an unparalleled record. The creation of the Dundas of the day as a Lord of Session, as 'Lord Arniston', became such a regular event that the peerage might just as well have become hereditary.

The second Lord Arniston had spent some time in Holland, where, like so many exiled Scottish landowners, he became enthused by grand ideas concerning European Renaissance architecture. On his return to Arniston after the 'Glorious Revolution' of 1688, when he entered public life as an

MP for Midlothian, he began making improvements, particularly in the gardens. Eventually, in 1725, he engaged William Adam to build a new house.

By the time of the old Judge's death the next year, though, the building work had progressed no further than the demolition of the enclosing walls of the gardens. It was left to his second son, another Lord Arniston, to proceed with the Adam project. He had risen with extraordinary rapidity to become first Solicitor-General and then Lord Advocate in his father's lifetime. On inheriting Arniston in 1726, he pressed on with Adam's building work.

Adam partly based his plans on what was already *in situ*. Thus the old house also had a range of buildings which grouped round the main block much as the present pavilions do now. The main hall of the present house incorporates part of the older house, whereas the Oak Room at the back remains as a highly evocative reminder of the 17th-century at Arniston. This atmospheric panelled chamber was one of Sir Walter Scott's favourite interiors. 'I have always loved the old Oak Room at Arniston', reminisced the author of *The Heart of Midlothian*, 'where I have drunk many a bottle and where I have seen many a hare killed.'

PRECEDING PAGES
The south (garden) front.
The coat of arms in the
pediment was rescued in
the early 1800s from the
Old Parliament House in
Edinburgh by Robert
Dundas, the fifth
successive head of his
family to rise to the
bench of the Supreme
Court of Scotland.

LEFT
As it was: the romantic
ruin of the John Adam
Drawing Room, ravaged
by dry rot in the 1950s.
Recently it has been
triumphantly restored,
with the plasterwork
reinstated and with
Chinese decorative paper
much admired by visitors
to this increasingly
sought-after showplace.

The first part of the new house to be tackled was the Hall, with its spectacular plasterwork by Joseph Enzer, a brilliant Dutch stuccoist whom William Adam was to employ on a number of houses including the House of Dun (see pages 134–43). Given a free hand to enclose the old baronial 'keep', Adam created an astonishing galleried interior which somehow succeeds in blending the Baroque, Classical and Rococo styles into a harmonious whole. So intensely dramatic is the composition that one experiences difficulty in taking it all in at once; every angle affords a striking new perspective.

Initially the building work went along at a steady rate. Unfortunately, though, the cost of Wiliam Adam's elaborate formal gardens – which culminated in a white-stone cascade on the hill behind the house – rather ran away with the budget and in the early 1730s matters came to an abrupt halt, with the west third of the main block incomplete.

The third Lord Arniston, his first family soon to be devastated by smallpox, was in no mood to carry on. The strains of bringing up a new family of nine with his second wife put paid to the prospect of any more expensive architectural indulgencies, even though he attained the highest office in the Judiciary as Lord President of the Court of Session. His son and namesake, the fourth Lord Arniston, who survived the smallpox epidemic through his absence abroad at Utrecht University, was also to achieve the same prize. Upon inheriting Arniston in 1753, he discovered that the estate was in a great deal of debt. Happily, his first wife, Henrietta Carmichael, was an heiress and her fortune was used to finish off the house.

The architect chosen for the task was William Adam's son John. He altered his father's plans for the internal layout of the uncompleted part of the house by arranging for rooms to be constructed on only two floors instead of three, while keeping within the original façade. This resulted in a splendid Drawing Room and Dining Room.

Alas, as Althea Dundas Bekker pointed out, the state of affairs in the early 1990s was that 'Arniston had gone back almost to the 1730s situation'. An outbreak of dry rot in the 1950s had led to the John Adam rooms being stripped of the internal plasterwork and all affected timber, leaving only the external shell. Yet it is splendid to report that by the end of the 20th century both the Dining Room and then the Drawing Room were triumphantly restored, with the help of grants from Historic Scotland, the national conservation agency.

The fourth Lord Arniston's son, another Robert (who became Lord Chief Baron of the Exchequer), was the fifth successive head of the family to rise to the bench of the Supreme Court, but declined the Lord Presidency on the grounds of poor health. He did much to improve the Arniston estate, which he adorned with stonework rescued from the demolished Old Parliament House in the early 1800s, and was also responsible for inserting the Scottish coat-of-arms in the pediment on the south side of Arniston House.

The porch on the north side was added in the 1860s by the Chief Baron's grandson, Sir Robert Dundas, 1st Bt, who also heightened the colonnades linking the pavilions to the main part of the house. Inside, he introduced many practical modern conveniences, as well as creating the new ground-floor Library and replacing the stone floor of the Hall with parquet.

In more recent times Arniston has been dogged by bad luck. The roof of the main block had to be completely renewed in the 1980s, the steps leading to the south porch had to be restored and further outbreaks of the dreaded dry rot in various parts of the house have had to be tackled. 'Much work still remains to be done', admits Althea Dundas Bekker (the eldest daughter of Sir Philip Dundas, 4th Bt), who has been courageously battling away here since the 1970s.

Yet Arniston has the feel of a deeply loved house and we can only be confident of its prospects. It is abundantly full of fun and charm – from Victorian toys in the Old Nursery to the curious old clock in the Hall with its two little old men bashing out the chimes with their hammers.

THE HOUSE OF DUN

ANGUS

AS IN THE previous chapter on Arniston, the House of Dun, near Montrose, was designed by William Adam for a leading lawyer and adorned with exuberant plasterwork by Joseph Enzer. There, though, the similarity ends for this former seat of the Erskines (now the property of the National Trust for Scotland) does not fit so easily into the pigeon-hole of Classical country houses. The House of Dun is essentially an early 'villa', in the Roman as opposed to the suburban sense of that word, and an exceptionally rare piece of architecture. On these terms alone it demands inclusion among the great houses of Scotland, with the tenure of a colourful family and the recent sympathetic restoration by the National Trust adding lustre to its claims.

The Erskines acquired the estate, overlooking the Montrose Basin, in 1375. In the 16th century the 5th Laird, John Erskine, an associate of John Knox, became Moderator of the General Assembly of the Church of Scotland. He was described as 'a mild sweet-tempered man' by Mary Queen of Scots who found him preferable to most reformers. This may have accounted for his surviving the trip to Paris to attend Mary's wedding to the Dauphin of France; several of the other official commissioners in attendance are supposed to have been poisoned.

Poison certainly played a part in a vicious feud at Dun in the 17th century. Upon the succession of the young 10th Laird, John, in 1610, his wicked Uncle Robert and three demon aunts plotted to bump off both him and his younger brother, Alexander. The boys were administered the poisoned draught and, as a contemporary account recorded, an extraordinary bout of vomiting ensued, which was so severe that no one expected them to live. John's skin 'turned black and his inward parts were consumed. He continued in great pain and doller to the time of his death.' Uncle Robert

PRECEDING PAGES
The entrance front, with
the south bank of the
Montrose Basin in the
background.

LEFT
Martial doorway in
the Saloon.

RIGHT
A bas-relief of Mars
dominates the far wall of
the Saloon. The Roman
god of war stands
'guardant' above the
Scottish regalia.

and two of his sisters went to the block, while Aunt Helen ('mair peni-
tent though less giltie') was banished to Orkney.

    In the early 18th century the old tower-house – about a quarter of a
mile west of the present house – was still standing. By 1723, however, as
Alexander McGill noted, the old castle was 'Raze'd Dow'n to the Ground'.
McGill, the official Edinburgh City Architect, was commissioned by the then
Laird David Erskine – styled 'Lord Dun' as a Lord of Session – to draw
up plans for a new house.

These plans were then passed on to Lord Dun's architectural adviser, the 23rd Earl of Mar, better known as 'Bobbing John', the exiled Jacobite leader then living in France. Lord Dun looked up to him as the head of the Erskine family and, together with his friend Lord Grange (Bobbing John's brother), went so far as to buy the attainted Earl's estate, clear it of debt and then entail it on the Mar heirs. Bobbing John, who fancied himself as an amateur architect, delighted in pouring scorn over McGill's efforts. He considered McGill's design of the house more appropriate for 'a Burgher's near to a great town, than for a Gentleman's seat in the Country'.

Bobbing John countered with a grandiose scheme, incorporating a tree-lined canal 1,000 yards long. This proved too much even for the dutiful Lord Dun, though William Adam did borrow Bobbing John's idea of a monumental niche on the entrance front. This can be seen at the centre of the implied triumphal arch which gives the House of Dun its special character.

Adam appears to have based his design on the Château d'Issy, near Paris, which was built by Pierre Bullet for the Princesse de Conti. This building was very familiar to Lord Mar who encouraged Adam to tickle up his original design of 1730 to make it more ornamental. As it turned out, the intended balustrades and urn finials on the north and south fronts were not executed but, in an admirably bold move, the National Trust for Scotland has recently created and installed them, based on Adam's designs.

Majestic as the unusual exterior undoubtedly is, the highpoint of the House of Dun has to be the glorious plasterwork in the Saloon by Enzer, who also worked for William Adam at Arniston (see pages 124–33). One stands there quite overwhelmed by the sheer swagger of the assorted chunky trophies, armour and classical figures.

Subsequent Erskine Lairds tended to concentrate on agriculture and sport, none more so than the spinster 16th Laird, Alice Erskine, a woman of masculine habits who was prone to crashing around the country on her sturdy hunter with her ill-fitting red wig askew. She would usually be accompanied by a faithful old retainer, who had lost a hand in a shooting accident, brandishing a hook. Alice slept in a bedroom overlooking the stableyard so that she could bellow down to the stable lads and also oversee the duties of the henwife in the Hen House (happily extant with its original 18th-century nesting boxes).

Much-needed modernization was undertaken by her nephew, John Kennedy-Erskine (younger brother of the 2nd Marquess of Ailsa, of Culzean – see pages 170–77) and his wife, Lady Augusta. They opened up the hall with an arch leading to the staircase, and dismantled Lord Dun's library, which had occupied the big room over the Saloon. Lady Augusta, a

LEFT
View from Saloon into
Entrance Hall.

passionate botanist who lived on at the House of Dun for another 34 years after her husband's death in 1831, was a natural daughter of King William IV by the actress Mrs Jordan.

The third of Dun's redoubtable trio of women was Lady Augusta's granddaughter, the author and artist Violet Jacob, celebrated for her poem *The Sheep Stealers*. She was haunted by her memories of the House of Dun: 'The trees that shelter it on three sides give it a tremendous solemnity, and the associations that brood like a cloud of witnesses about it seem as much part of its life as the coming and going of latter-day feet.'

As the 20th century progressed, these brooding clouds came to dominate the House of Dun. The house was unsympathetically altered in 1912. Subsequently the 20th Laird ended his days in a psychiatric hospital and his spinster sister, Marjorie, committed suicide believing herself – according to the inquest – to be under the spell of a dealer in Black Magic. Their sister, Millicent Lovett, the 21st Laird, let out the House of Dun as a sporting hotel. William Adam's Parlour, which had been used as a smoking room in the 19th century, found itself called 'The Whips Bar'.

Finally, in 1980, Millicent Lovett, the last Laird, died and bequeathed the estate, house and contents to the National Trust for Scotland. The Trust's expert team of David Learmont, Christopher Hartley and John Batty did an invigorating job of restoring the place without turning it into a museum. The rooms, both 'upstairs' and 'downstairs', are full of vitality and

PRECEDING PAGES
William Adam's 'withdrawing room' which was given a colonnaded screen and enlarged into the present Dining Room in the early 19th century. The furniture was supplied by the Edinburgh cabinet-maker William Trotter in 1828. The marble chimneypiece is original William Adam.

LEFT
Detail of Joseph Enzer's plasterwork in the Saloon, showing a watchful Scottish lion.

ABOVE
The Entrance Hall, with
more plasterwork by
Enzer. The busts are
(*left*) Rear-Admiral
Adolphus FitzClarence
(by Samuel Joseph,
1854), a favourite
brother of Lady Augusta,
the châtelaine of Dun,
and (*right*) Lady
Augusta's son, William
Henry Kennedy-Erskine,
the 18th Laird (by
C.E. Fuller, 1857).

character. The Saloon has sensibly been made an uncluttered room of parade; the Dining Room hung with family portraits; the 'Whips Bar' ingeniously converted back to the Parlour; the Library re-created. Especially atmospheric are the Gun and Rod Rooms in the basement – gamily evocative of the Edwardian Laird and his sport – and the Kitchen, complete with copper *batterie de cuisine*.

Queen Elizabeth The Queen Mother, the National Trust for Scotland's Patron, came to tea at the House of Dun in May 1989 when she officially opened it to the public. Many visitors since have delighted in both the Trust's sensitive and unstuffy restoration of a fascinating architectural gem and the feeling nicely expressed by John Cornforth that 'they can imagine themselves on a visit to an elderly uncle or aunt, with solid meals in the dining room, a loyal but invisible staff and pleasurable fishing expeditions.'

HADDO HOUSE

ABERDEENSHIRE

ONE OF the hardest problems when preserving a country house is to avoid 'museumization'. As we have seen in the previous chapter, on the House of Dun (see pages 134-43), it can be done, but it is assuredly much easier to achieve when the family is still in residence. This is happily still the case at Haddo House, near Aberdeen, where June Marchioness of Aberdeen, widow of the 4th Marquess of Aberdeen and Temair (who made over the property to the NTS shortly before his death in 1974) and a live-wire personality in her own right, ensures that the place retains a strong family atmosphere.

The daughter of a decisive Headmaster of Harrow – where the Gordons, Earls and Marquesses of Aberdeen, have been educated for generations – the former June Boissier is a trained musician and a passionate champion of the arts. Together with her husband, David, the 4th Marquess, she developed the Haddo House Choral Society from small beginnings, as his brainchild, to become one of Scotland's major cultural ventures. Haddo has earned a reputation as a thriving centre for artistic endeavours; operas have been staged as well as seasons of plays. One creative visitor described Haddo as 'not so much a place as an experience'.

The building of the original Haddo House in the 1730s must have proved no less of an experience, even a shock, to the hardy folk of the Grampians used to bleak castles and tower-houses rather than elegant exercises in the Palladian manner. Hitherto the Gordons of Haddo (an estate acquired in 1469 from the Foulartons) had been content to live in the old 'Place of Kellie', though, according to one 17th-century account, this was no spartan affair but a sumptuously furnished house.

George Gordon, the 1st Earl of Aberdeen, despite being Lord High Chancellor of Scotland and making a prosperous marriage to a Lockhart

heiress, did not see the need to build a new pile for himself and died at
Kellie in 1720. His son and successor, William, the 2nd Earl, had grander
ideas. According to the witty account of the family in *A Wild Flight of
Gordons* by Archie Gordon (otherwise the bachelor 5th Marquess of Aberdeen),
the 2nd Earl was 'ambitious, financially accumulative and a thumping snob'.

Besides marrying first the daughter of an Earl (Leven and Melville) and
then the daughters of two Dukes (Atholl and Gordon), William expanded
the estates considerably and consulted Sir John Clerk of Penicuik, the
Palladian pundit, about creating a suitable new seat. Clerk recommended
the services of William Adam (who else?) as architect and John Baxter,
who had just finished work on Clerk's own villa of Mavisbank, as the mason
to supervise the building work.

They did not hang around. First of all, Baxter demolished the old house
of Kellie in the spring of 1732 and by that autumn the new building, on the

PRECEDING PAGES
The entrance front.

ABOVE
The comfortable
Drawing Room, which
retains its 1880
decorative scheme.
The chandelier and
most of the furniture
were supplied by Wright
& Mansfield. Above
the fireplace is
Domenichino's study
of David, the slayer of
Goliath.

The even cosier Morning Room, also redecorated in the 1880s during the reign of 'We Twa' (as the 1st Marquess and his wife, the former Ishbel Marjoribanks, called themselves). Previously, in the time of the 4th Earl of Aberdeen, it had been a library.

same site, was as high as the second storey. A year later, the house was 'now near Roffed' with timber from Norway.

Unfortunately, the 2nd Earl of Aberdeen's successor, 'the Wicked Earl', did not greatly care for his father's spanking new house and preferred to expend his not inconsiderable energies elsewhere. Archie Gordon pithily sums him up: 'He neglected Haddo House and its châtelaine, loved his extra-marital families, especially those at Ellon [a castle not far from Haddo], was very smart at the business of making his estates pay for his heavy commitments, and referred to himself as "us".' The châtelaine he neglected was a former cook at a Yorkshire inn – where the Wicked Earl put up in 1759. The story goes that he so enjoyed the mutton chops there that he insisted on complimenting the tender of the stove in person – whom he found no less succulent. On his next visit the doughty cook, brandishing pistols, demanded marriage or his life.

LEFT

Rounding the corner *en route* for the Library.

RIGHT

The Library, another splendid room of the 1880s (converted from haylofts over the stables), with cedar woodwork inlaid with ebony. The marble chimneypiece contains copies of Wedgwood jasperware plaques taken from an original in Brook House.

The Wicked Earl also neglected the education of his eventual heir, George, who was left virtually penniless by the early deaths of his parents, Lord and Lady Haddo, in the 1790s. Being an enterprising lad, though, young George, stranded in London, enlisted the help of a fellow Scot, Viscount Melville. The Prime Minister, William Pitt, also agreed to act as one of the boy's curators, and memorably reproved the Wicked Earl for his negligence, with the dry observation that he 'did not concur with his Lordship in considering that rank superseded the necessity for education'.

George was duly sent to Harrow and Cambridge where he distinguished himself as a Classical scholar. Lord Byron (a kinsman and fellow Harrovian) sang of him in *English Bards and Scotch Reviewers* as 'the travelled thane, Athenian Aberdeen'. He soon made his mark in politics and after stints as Foreign and Colonial Secretary became Prime Minister himself in 1852. Three years later he had to resign after the Coalition he led was blamed for the mismanagement of the Crimean War; but, as *The Times* obituary was to point out, Lord Aberdeen 'belonged to that class of statesman who are great without being brilliant, who succeed without ambition, who without eloquence become famous, who retain their power even when deprived of place.'

At Haddo he commissioned the local architect Archibald Simpson to raise by a storey the curved corridors which join the central block to the wings. The southern wing (which housed the domestic offices) was enlarged around an office court, terminating in a clock tower with cupola. Outside, the 4th Earl laid out a grass terrace and a double lime avenue beyond it, to the east, and employed James Giles to supervise the planting of thousands of trees and the formation of a chain of three lakes in the park. To celebrate his installation as a Knight of the Garter in 1855 he inserted an elaborate armorial panel above the central Drawing Room window which led to the terrace. Queen Victoria, who had granted him the very rare distinction of being permitted to retain the Thistle as well as the Garter, came to stay at Haddo two years later.

Later in the 19th century the 7th Earl of Aberdeen was Governor-General of Canada, Viceroy of Ireland and promoted to a Marquessate. His formidable wife, Ishbel Marjoribanks, was not initially impressed by Haddo – 'Why have you brought me to this horrible house?' she enquired of her husband – and promptly set about a radical programme of improvements which largely shaped the house we see today. The south wing was converted into family rooms; an austere Gothic chapel was built to the designs of G.E. Street; and the Edinburgh architects, Wardrop & Reid, created a new ground-floor entrance hall and associated staircases on the west front. This spoilt the Palladian purity of the principal elevation, though it undoubtedly enhanced Haddo's comfortable atmosphere.

The 1st Marquess of Aberdeen and his wife liked referring to themselves as 'We Twa' (indeed they published two volumes entitled *We Twa* and *More Cracks with We Twa*), rather in the way the Wicked Earl called himself 'us'. There was, though, nothing wicked about We Twa, who devoted themselves to philanthropic and charitable works which had a deleterious effect on the family fortunes. Fortunately the 4th Marquess, who took over the running of the estate at the end of the Second World War, was a trained land agent and a far-sighted polymath who secured the house's future by arranging for it to be cared for by the National Trust for Scotland.

DUFF HOUSE

BANFFSHIRE

BY THE 1970s, art galleries, caught in the vice-like grip of the 'Modern' Movement, had become depressing affairs. Historic pictures, many of which had once hung in great country houses, were unimaginatively displayed under strip-lights on stark walls in soulless spaces. Much of the credit for the transformation of such anti-historical interiors into aesthetically appropriate settings for works of art must go to the enthusiastic Tim Clifford, who became Director of the National Galleries of Scotland in 1984.

As well as breathing new life into the main galleries in Edinburgh, which suddenly became full of vigour with pictures hung as they would be in a family house against a robust background of richly coloured walls and surrounded by furniture and *objets d'art* which delighted the eye, Clifford also encouraged the setting-up of 'outstations', whereby parts of the national collections could be shown in country houses. Principal among these is undoubtedly Duff House – an astonishing and hitherto all too little-known Baroque pile wedged between two small seaside towns, Macduff and Banff, in one of north-east Scotland's dimmest counties.

Some ten years ago Duff was, to say the least, a 'problem' house. In the course of the 20th century this former treasure-house of the Duffs, Earls and Dukes of Fife, had been variously a sanatorium for sufferers from habitual constipation ('disorders of nutrition, excluding inebriation', as the brochure tactfully put it), a prisoner-of-war camp and a troops billet. In 1956 the Ministry of Works, concerned at the fate of 'this fine example of architecture in the grand manner', took Duff under its wing and carried out essential repairs. It was even opened to the public on a very limited scale.

In 1988 the official organization then responsible for Duff, Historic Buildings and Monuments (later to become 'Historic Scotland'), called a

public meeting to try to find a suitable role for the house. Eventually, at a second meeting, the enterprising Tim Clifford came up with a solution to the problem. The proposal was that the National Galleries would not only provide pictures for the house but also endeavour to find suitable furnishings.

Happily, his scheme won the day and in the 1990s, thanks to an unprecedented partnership between Historic Scotland (which contributed £2 million to the restoration of the fabric), the National Galleries of Scotland, Grampian Regional Council, Banff and Buchan District Council, and with assistance from Grampian Enterprise Ltd, Duff was indeed restored to much of its former glory. Nearly all the pictures now hanging at Duff House were sought out from the National Galleries' own reserves. 'The pictures', explains Tim Clifford, 'have not been chosen for their "star" quality – although there are many stars amongst them – but to furnish appropriately a great aristocratic country house.' Quite rightly, Clifford makes no apology for the preponderance of portraits, because that is what has always hung here.

Indeed in its heyday, the late 18th century, Duff was not so dissimilar to the country-house gallery it has become today. For the 2nd Earl Fife, a Fellow of both the Royal Society and the Society of Antiquaries, was a celebrated connoisseur and a pioneer collector of portraits on his-

torical lines. The upper rooms at Duff were completed in the 1790s in order to display his ever-expanding picture collection.

Duff had been built by the 2nd Earl's father, when Lord Braco, to the designs of William Adam. These prompted John Cornforth of *Country Life* to enthuse about 'echoes of Castle Howard and surely of Houghton, too; of Hawksmoor, particularly at Easton Neston; and of Gibbs, in its plan and ornaments.' Yet the wonderfully flamboyant Duff could, as Cornforth says, 'only be a Scottish building, in its height, strength and upward thrust'. An instructive model on show at Duff shows that Adam's original intention was to set off the towering central block with quadrant colonnades

BELOW
Stairwell.

RIGHT
View through to the
Great Staircase from
the Vestibule.

and two flanking wings. This was to be the Duff family's triumphant expression of their magnate status.

In the event, the wings were never built, and the fitting-up of the interior was abandoned after a corking row between patron and architect ended up in the Law Courts. To the fury of the 1st Earl Fife (as Lord Braco became in 1739 when the shell of the house was complete) William Adam overcharged for the stonemasons' work and the architect was obliged to sue for parts of his costs.

The completion of the interior was left to the 2nd Earl Fife. First, in the late 1750s, came the first floor (always intended to be for daily living). The Dining Room is a particularly pleasing example from this period of decoration, with its carved panelling, pilasters and a *papier-mâché* ceiling. Then, in the 1780s, the 2nd Earl constructed the main staircase before completing the two big rooms on the second floor (planned by Adam for State).

Further redecoration was carried out by the 4th Earl Fife, a former Major-General in the Spanish Army who had fought with the future Duke of Wellington in the Peninsular War and was another collector of pictures. John Jackson's stencil painting in the Vestibule and Great Staircase dates from the 4th Earl's time.

The last principal stage of decoration was done by the wife of the 5th Earl, the former Lady Agnes Hay, in the 1860s before she died as a result of a fall from her carriage. It was she who enriched the North Drawing Room and added gilding to some of the other interiors. Lady Agnes's mother, Lady Elizabeth FitzClarence, was an illegitimate daughter of King William IV and later in the 19th century Duff acquired an even stronger royal connection when Lady Agnes's son, the 6th Earl Fife, married Princess Louise, the future Princess Royal, eldest daughter of the Prince of Wales (later King Edward VII), who stayed at Duff in 1883. Two days after the wedding, in July 1889, Queen Victoria created her grandson-in-law Duke of Fife.

Although David Bryce had added a new kitchen and bedroom wing in 1870 for the 5th Earl, Duff proved less appealing to the new royal chatelaine than a rebuilt Mar Lodge close to Balmoral. And so in 1906 the Duke of Fife, by then in financial difficulties, presented Duff House, plus 140 acres, to the burgh of Banff and one of William Adam's greatest architectural achievements rather disappeared from view.

Today, though, it has bounced back into life. As well as the splendid architecture, with the turret-like pavilions and façades richly ornamented by pilasters, pediments and urns, one can enjoy a feast of good pictures (such as El Greco's *St Jerome in Penitence*, J.G. Cuyp's Dutch family group, panels by Francois Boucher and portraits dominated by Allan Ramsay's full-length study of *Mrs Daniel Cunyngham*) and some magnificent furniture.

RIGHT
The Dining Room, a handsome interior of the 1750s, with a *papier-mâché* ceiling installed for the 2nd Earl Fife in 1761. The mahogany table came from Dunimarle, Fife; the gilt-bronzed candelabra are after a design by C.H. Tatham (1801) and were made by Storr & Mortimer for the 4th Earl Fife.

LEFT
The Great Staircase.

RIGHT
The North Drawing Room, notable for its sumptuous suite of gilded furniture (complete with original case covers in blue linen damask and crimson piping) from the collection of Cardinal Fesch, Archbishop of Paris and Lyons, who is said to have been given the pieces by his step-nephew, the Emperor Napoleon.

Especially impressive are the suites said to have been given by Napoleon to his step-uncle, Cardinal Fesch, which are on loan from the Magdalene Sharpe Erskine Trust of Dunimarle, Culross, Fife. The Marquess of Zetland has lent a superb suite of furniture made by Thomas Chippendale to the design of Robert Adam.

The new Duff House only opened its doors in 1995 and, as Tim Clifford says, these are still early days in the long campaign to furnish it completely. Yet already plenty of visitors are bringing back excited reports that Duff is a delightful discovery, reflecting a new dawn in the intelligent celebration of the country house as a lively temple of the arts.

INVERARAY CASTLE

ARGYLL

THE FAMILY seat of the Campbells, Dukes of Argyll, nicely encapsulates their role in developing the Western Highlands and Islands for the British Crown without losing faith with the essential Scottish spirit embodied in the proud title of *Mac Cailein Mor*, Chief of the Clan. For while Inveraray Castle was designed by an English architect (the Palladian Roger Morris) and neatly placed in an idealized and reclaimed landscape, complete with model town, its rugged mountainous setting beside the haunting waters of Loch Fyne is inescapably Gaelic.

Indeed the family history of the Campbells is effectively the history of Scotland. The Duke of Argyll is one of the few Highland Chiefs in the old Peerage of Scotland. His ancestors became Earls in the 15th century, when they moved their headquarters from the freshwater of Loch Awe to the seawater of Loch Fyne; rising to a Marquessate in the 17th century, when the 1st (and only) Marquess abandoned the traditional Campbell loyalty to the Stuarts and led the Covenanters in the Civil War; and finally to a Dukedom in 1701, when King William III rewarded his faithful lieutenant in the 'Glorious Revolution'.

The 2nd Duke of Argyll, one of the first two Field Marshals to be created in the British Army, followed his father in being a staunch anti-Jacobite. Not long after the first Rising – or 'Rebellion', as he would have described it – the 2nd Duke considered a grandiose scheme by Sir John Vanbrugh to build a new castle on the bank of the Aray. The 15th-century tower-house there was crumbling away and the Duke, who, according to Horace Walpole had 'a head admirably turned to mechanics', must have been tempted. In the event, though, he preferred to pursue his passion for planting in England; it was left to his brother, Archibald, to start the great project.

PRECEDING PAGES
The stupendous Armoury Hall, devised by Anthony Salvin after the fire of 1877 and recent repainted.

LEFT
The Saloon, appliqués gilded by Maitland Bogg of Edinburgh (1788); Thomas Gainsborough's portrait of Field Marshal Henry Seymour-Conway, Secretary of State for the Northern Department and son-in-law of the 4th Duke of Argyll; and sofa gilded by Dupasquier (1782).

RIGHT
The garden front of the castle.

Duke Archibald did not come into the estates until 1743 when he was 61. Yet nothing – not even Inveraray's extraordinary remoteness at that time – was going to stop him from realizing the dream of creating not only a new castle but a new setting too. The old town that abutted the old castle was to be swept away and rebuilt on a new site, the surrounding land transformed into a nobleman's park.

The new castle, adapted by Morris from the original sketch by Vanbrugh and tricked up with the newly fashionable Gothick ornament, was intended to contrast its symmetry against the wildness of the landscape. Although the architect was seldom able to visit the site, William Adam kept an eye on the building operations and work proceeded as best it could considering the handicaps of transport and such local difficulties as the 1745 Jacobite Rising. The walls and roof were up within ten years and the structure was completed in 1758.

Unfortunately, Duke Archibald was never able to occupy the new castle. By the time Dr Johnson came to Inveraray in 1773, though, it was fully occupied, with the 5th Duke of Argyll, another Field Marshal, and his family comfortably installed. His wife Elizabeth, a celebrated beauty of the Court of King George III, treated Dr Johnson kindly, though studiously ignored his travelling companion, James Boswell. Dr Johnson

was impressed enough by the unusual slate-like stone (from Creggans, on the other side of Loch Fyne) of the castle but felt it would look better if raised by an additional storey.

The 5th Duke, though, had his own ideas for improvements. Robert Mylne, scion of a dynasty of master masons who had been employed by the Kings of Scots since the 15th century, was brought in to re-cast the interiors in the 1780s. The windows were lengthened to reach floor level and the main entrance was switched from the south to the north, where a former gallery was divided up into an entrance hall and rooms either side.

The Dining Room and the Drawing Room were redecorated in a French style made newly fashionable by the Prince of Wales (the future King George IV) at Carlton House in London. The Prince's exquisite creation did not survive for long so this makes the Inveraray interiors all the more important, though 'important' seems far too dull a word to describe such gay and ravishing confections with their *grisailles* by Guinand and floral ornamentation by Girard (who worked at Carlton House).

Robert Mylne also busied himself outside the castle: he was responsible for designing the stable quadrangle, known as Cherry Park, the Aray Bridge, and much of the model new town, including the church. The 5th Duke of Argyll tended to devote his energies to improving the town rather than the castle after his beloved Duchess Elizabeth died in 1790.

In the 19th century Dr Johnson's wish for Inveraray was partly fulfilled, as the result of a disastrous fire in 1877. The upper floors were gutted and as a consequence the battlements were removed and dormer windows superimposed. To make those changes the 8th Duke of Argyll, a prominent Liberal politician, consulted Anthony Salvin, the Victorian castle specialist, who could not resist adding the jolly conical roofs on the corner towers.

Although the State rooms escaped the fire of 1877, the central tower was gutted and Salvin redesigned it as an Armoury Hall. The displays of weaponry, fantastically piled in wheels and fans, includes 'Brown Bess' muskets that were used in the '45 Rising, Lochaber axes and fearsome Highland broadswords. The arms stretching upwards in the 70-foot-high tower make an astonishing impact on the visitor.

Shortly before the fire, the 8th Duke of Argyll's eldest son and heir, the Marquess of Lorne, strengthened the family's close links to the Crown by marrying Princess Louise, Queen Victoria's fourth – and most beautiful – daughter. The Victoria Room at Inveraray contains the maplewood writing desk given by Queen Victoria to Princess Louise (who became a talented sculptress) on her marriage in 1871. The occasion was marked at the castle by the construction of an elaborate glass and iron-covered entrance

PRECEDING PAGES
The State Dining Room:
perhaps the finest
painted room in Britain.
The French decorative
painters were Girard and
Guinand, whose work
only survives at
Inveraray. The chandelier
is Waterford, *circa* 1830;
the silver-gilt *nefs*, or
sailing ships are German,
circa 1900. The portrait
over the fireplace is of
the 4th Duke of Argyll,
in his Coronation robes.

LEFT
Detail of painted panels.

bridge to the design of Matthew Digby Wyatt. In the early 1890s Inveraray
became the first house to be installed with electricity in Scotland.

Lord Lorne, who became the 9th Duke of Argyll, died childless and
his successor, the 10th Duke, was a bachelor so Inveraray remained virtually untouched for the first half of the 20th century. Then, with the help
of the distinguished architect Ian Lindsay, the 11th Duke carried out a sympathetic restoration of both the castle and the town. The castle had fallen
prey to dry and wet rot and had to be rewired, re-roofed, re-floored, re-fen-
estrated and comprehensively repaired before it could be opened to the
public in 1953.

ABOVE
Bird's-eye view of the
model town of Inveraray
on the shores of Loch
Fyne.

Shortly after the present Duke of Atholl succeeded to Inveraray 20 years later, though, disaster struck again. Another fire, nearly a century on from the previous one, broke out in November 1975. The castle was gutted in the conflagration, but admirably swift action managed to save the State rooms once more, and most of the contents. With determination and drive, the present Duke and his Duchess, formerly Miss Iona Colquhoun of Luss, set about making good the damage. The building was repaired with remarkable dispatch, the painted rooms restored, the tapestries cleaned.

More recently, a comprehensive new restoration scheme has been undertaken: a mammoth project involving some 20 tonnes of scaffolding in the central towers. All the arms, pictures and tapestries came down and went into store while the conservation team devoted themselves to relining, pointing and plastering, as well as painting the house in the authentic 18th-century manner. The result is that, at the dawn of a new Millennium, Inveraray is indeed a fitting showplace for the headquarters of the Clan Campbell and is the epitome of the Anglo-Scottish experience at its best.

CULZEAN CASTLE

AYRSHIRE

THE SEA, the sea.... Of all the great houses of Scotland benefiting from a maritime position, none can match Culzean Castle, perched on a clifftop above the Ayrshire coastline, for sheer spectacle and drama. Robert Adam's romantic creation for the Kennedys, Earls of Cassillis (and later Marquesses of Ailsa), now the flagship property of the National Trust for Scotland, enjoys views that are without rival in Europe. You look out from the windows and battlements of the 18th-century castle across the Firth of Clyde to the mountains of Arran, while to the left the brooding Ailsa Craig, a rocky island rising to 1,114 feet, looms out of the sea.

The Kennedy family had been seated hereabouts since medieval times, Culzean being only one of a dozen small castles in their hands as they rose to be the most prominent landowning dynasty in Ayrshire. The 4th Earl of Cassillis's brother, Sir Thomas Kennedy of Culzean (murdered on the Sands of Ayr in 1602), was the ancestor of the line of Kennedys that were to improve and extend the castle.

Originally Culzean was a comparatively modest Scots tower-house, with an 'L'-shaped tower, vaulted service quarters on the ground floor, a single great hall occupying the whole of the first floor and a cluster of private apartments on the floors above. By the end of the 17th century it had ceased to be a purely defensive fortress and, according to a description of 1693, was 'flanked on the south with very pretty gardens and orchards, adorned with excellent tarrases'. These 'tarrases' and 'two dainty spring wells' in the caves hollowed out of the rock are the two oldest surviving features at Culzean.

It was Sir Thomas's bachelor descendant and namesake who in 1762, after a lengthy legal dispute, established his right to succeed as the

9th Earl of Cassillis. An 'improving laird', the 9th Earl had been busy enclosing the Culzean estate and in 1760 had added a new wing to the old
castle that stretched to the edge of the cliff. Naturally enough, he preferred to remain at Culzean rather than move to the then principal seat of
the Kennedys, Cassillis House.

His brother David, another bachelor who succeeded as 10th Earl of
Cassillis in 1775, took a similar view and concentrated his energies on improving Culzean still further. The farm manager, John Bulley, greatly increased
the profits of the estate and the new Earl decided to make a big splash by
bringing in the most celebrated architect of the day, Robert Adam (who had
previously designed a new parish kirk at Kirkoswald for his brother).

Between 1777 and 1792 the irrepressible Adam radically rebuilt Culzean
Castle in four stages. First, he 'squared up' the old tower house into the
great south front – overlooking the 'tarrases' – and added a three-storey
wing on either side. Some of the masonry of the old tower was incorporated
within the central block. Adam also built a new kitchen block at the east end
of the 9th Earl's wing, and the wing itself was modified. However, not content with all this tinkering about, Adam then proceeded to knock down the
9th Earl's wing in 1785. In its place, between the kitchen block and the
brewhouse, rose the mighty Drum Tower, with rooms on either side of
it. The Saloon, the principal room in the Drum Tower, gave Adam the opportunity, brilliantly grasped, of contrasting the characteristics of 18th-century
elegance with the wild scenery of sea, sky and mountain irresistibly framed
in the windows.

Having taken Culzean Castle to the very edge of the cliff and gone
a long way to unifying the building, Adam had, nonetheless, not finished
yet. There was a space in the centre; he had forgotten to give the castle a
grand staircase in the central well. What was to be done? In order to
create enough room for his 1787 plans for the Oval Staircase he had to
pull down the 'back half' of the tower-house. By a stroke of genius he
managed to transform what had been a gloomy space into the central
interior of the castle.

The decoration of the interior carried on until 1795, three years
after Adam died. The great architect had designed almost everything the eye
could see – furniture and fittings, tables, mirrors, sconces and carpets. Outside, he had busied himself to build the stables enclosing the forecourt,
the home farm on the next headland up the coast and the romantic mock
ruined arch and causeway which now formed the principal approach to
the castle.

Understandably all this activity took its toll on the 10th Earl of
Cassillis, a martyr to gout. 'I hope', he wrote to his doubtless concerned

PRECEDING PAGES
The Oval Staircase:
Adam's afterthought.

ABOVE

The Dining Room,
originally planned as two
rooms – a library and a
dressing room – but
thrown into one during
the 1870s alterations of
Wardrop & Reid for the
3rd Marquess of Ailsa.

banker in 1790, 'my operations will [soon] be at an end for I am really
wearied of Building and wish to be at rest.' In the event, he died the
same year as his architect, in 1792. Together they had achieved a masterpiece.

Culzean then acquired an American connection, which has remained
strong to this day, when the Earldom of Cassillis passed to a kinsman,
Captain Archibald Kennedy, RN. He had retired from the Navy to No.1
Broadway, New York, where his father had been Collector of Customs –
though during the War of American Independence his house was requisi-

tioned by none other than George Washington. The American Earl's son and successor, another Archibald, was a friend of the bluff 'Sailor King', William IV (one of whose illegitimate daughters, Lady Augusta FitzClarence, married the Earl's second son, John Kennedy-Erskine of the House of Dun). The King created the Earl Marquess of Ailsa for his Coronation in 1831.

For all its splendour, Culzean had been built for a Georgian bachelor and in Victorian times the 3rd Marquess of Ailsa found it too cramped for his large family. Messrs Wardrop & Reid were duly summoned to build the west wing, on the site of Adam's brewhouse, in 1879. It was the 3rd Marquess's second son, the childless 5th Marquess of Ailsa, who, in 1945, offered Culzean and its glorious 560-acre 'policies' to the National Trust for Scotland.

BELOW
A corner of Robert Adam's peerless circular Saloon. The Louis XVI chairs are covered in Beauvais tapestry

RIGHT
The Armoury, mostly comprising weapons issued to the West Lowland Fencible Regiment when it was raised in the early 1800s.

ABOVE
The wild romanticicism of the scenery outside Culzean contrasts thrillingly with the cool Classical inside.

LEFT
The garden front of the castle and the viaduct framed by Robert Adam's 'ruined' arch.

Looking back, one is struck by the Trust's courage in taking it on. At the time many thought the gamble not so much courageous as foolhardy. Here, after half-a-dozen years of war and in an era of austerity when there was nothing like today's support for such ventures, was this tiny voluntary conservation agency (total membership 1,200; total free funds £5,000) accepting an unendowed historic property into inalienable care 'for the benefit of the nation'. The question was whether it would make or break the NTS.

It made the Trust. This extraordinary act of faith was to have immense significance in the history of the Heritage movement for at Culzean the NTS enterprisingly demonstrated the need for new legislation, agencies and techniques which have borne wider fruit. In the 1950s Culzean was among the first beneficiaries of grants made by the Historic Buildings Council set up by the Historic Buildings and Ancient Monuments Act of 1953. In the 1960s Culzean became Scotland's first 'Country Park', complete with ranger service, young naturalists' club, a treetop walkway, deer park and visitors' centre in Adam's old home-farm buildings.

The American links with Culzean have been a vital element in the National Trust for Scotland's fundraising. These were strengthened after the Second World War when the 5th Marquess of Ailsa asked that the Trust present General Eisenhower, Supreme Commander of the Allied Forces in Europe, with a flat in the top of the castle for his lifetime. A special exhibition commemorating Ike, and his visits to Culzean, is one of the many attractions that have made Culzean such a deservedly popular showplace. It is a triumphant example of the precept laid down by the stalwarts of the NTS, Sir Jamie Stormonth Darling and Robin Prentice, in their publication *Culzean: The Continuing Challenge*: 'If the decision is right, the money will follow'.

GOSFORD HOUSE

EAST LOTHIAN

MORE SEA, more Robert Adam. Yet at Gosford in East Lothian the maritime views seem not to have been as significant to the new house's patron, the 7th Earl of Wemyss, as the need to be closer to his beloved golf links; and Adam's original building has been much altered over the last two centuries – partly by other architectural hands and partly by a disastrous fire during the Second World War. Nonetheless, Gosford House, which remains the home of the present Earl of Wemyss, is an interesting example of Adam's later work (it was begun in 1790, only two years before his death), while William Young's late 19th-century Italianate south wing contains an astounding Marble Hall that must rank as one of Scotland's grandest interiors.

Although today James Ramsay's Picturesque late 18th-century 'pleasure ground' at Gosford, linked by a series of ponds, is regarded as one of the best surviving examples of this landscape style in Scotland (and has recently been sympathetically restored), the Golfing Earl's choice of situation on the wasteland adjoining the Firth of Forth between Longniddry and Aberlady excited the scorn of his contemporaries. The precocious 5th Duke of Rutland, up here on a visit in 1796, found it 'objectionable in the highest degree: a barren rabbit warren on a sandy shore stretching on all sides and the country around being totally destitute of wood or fertilization.'

Nor did the architecture please all comers. In 1799 Louisa Stuart, daughter-in-law of the Prime Minister Earl of Bute, observed: 'There is a *corps-de-logis* and two great pavilions, all with domes, so at a distance it looks like three great ovens but the front is really a very pretty one. They say the plan is absurd; three rooms in the middle of [a front] 50 feet long,

PRECEDING PAGES
The east (garden) front,
with the south wing in
the foreground.

LEFT
Corner of Marble Hall:
Italian marble, Caen
stone and alabaster.

RIGHT
The magnificent Marble
Hall in the Italianate
south wing built by
William Young for the
10th Earl of Wemyss in
the 1880s.

each lined with one huge Venetian window and unconnected with the rest'.

In fairness to Robert Adam, it should be emphasized that after his death those windows were enlarged out of all proportion at the insistence of the Golfing Earl, who wanted as much light as possible to show off his collection of Dutch and English pictures. Indeed the only unaltered part of Robert Adam's design at Gosford is the typically elegant stable block, some 300 yards to the east of the main house.

The house was completed in 1800, though in fact the Golfing Earl never took up residence because he is said to have found it too damp. Similarly, his grandson and successor, the 8th Earl of Wemyss, preferred

to stay put at Amisfield nearby, or at Old Gosford House, a 17th-century building (which was to be enlarged by the architect William Burn in the 1830s).

The Amisfield estate had been inherited by the Golfing Earl from his maternal family of Charteris. His father, the 5th Earl of Wemyss, had eloped with Janet, only child and heiress of the rich rake Colonel Francis Charteris of Amisfield. 'No woman', according to a stern footnote in *The Complete Peerage*, 'was safe' from the notorious Colonel (featured in Hogarth's *Harlot's Progress*), who was once sentenced to death for rape, but escaped the block.

The Colonel had acquired extensive estates which passed on his death in 1732 to his son-in-law on condition that he changed his name from Wemyss to Charteris. Although he was the second son of the 5th Earl of Wemyss, the new Mr Charteris eventually succeeded as *de jure* 7th Earl in

1786 and the ancestral Wemyss Castle estate in Fife passed to a younger brother, James. Today Wemyss remains the seat of the cadet branch of the family.

Meanwhile, back at Gosford, the 8th Earl of Wemyss toyed with the idea of radically altering his grandfather's house and consulted various architects, including the Classicist Sir Robert Smirke and possibly James Wyatt, then in his Gothic phase. In the event, he used none of their plans and contented himself with pulling down Adam's flanking pavilions, or wings, leaving the centre block in solitary state for more than 50 years.

The 9th Earl of Wemyss – known as 'the Hunting Earl' and the dedicatee of *Mr Sponge's Sporting Tour* by R.S. Surtees – was in favour of pulling the place down altogether, but was dissuaded from this drastic action by his more aesthetically minded son and successor. John Ruskin, no less, described the 10th Earl of Wemyss as having 'a genuine devotion to art' and as 'an

BELOW
The Gallery, top-lit to show off the great Dutch and Italian picture collections formed by the 7th and 10th Earls of Wemyss respectively.

amateur artist of considerable skill'. His legendary charm comes across in his *Memories*. Of his wedding reception in Vienna, for example, he records that the hotel cook carved an ice in the shape of a rabbit – 'emblematic, perhaps, of a numerous progeny and of the family home, Gosford, founded on a rabbit warren'. He and his bride, Lady Anne Anson, daughter of the 1st Earl of Lichfield, duly produced a brood of nine and it was to house them, and his beloved pictures, in style that he commissioned the architect William Young to remodel Gosford.

The 10th Earl had a lifelong passion for collecting pictures, with a particular leaning towards the Italian Renaissance. He was blessed with a superb 'eye' – and a flair for spotting a bargain. His first purchase was a Carlo Dolci from a pawnbroker in London, and on his first visit to Italy in 1842 he acquired two beautiful paintings from the proprietor of a café. Above all,

Lord Wemyss was a genuine collector, who purchased pictures that he admired regardless of the vagaries of fashion, and did not employ agents – indeed he disapproved of any collector who 'bought through other men's eyes and paid through his own nose'.

To show off his masterpieces by Botticelli, Murillo, Rubens and the rest, Lord Wemyss chose an architect who had made his mark with his successful design for the War Office in London and had just won the competition for the new City Chambers in Glasgow. The Marble Hall at Gosford, a grand vision of pink alabaster, Caen stone and plasterwork, rises to a height of three storeys. A magnificent double staircase ascends to a surrounding gallery separated from the hall by a screen of Venetian windows reminiscent of Robert Adam's original design for the west front. The central dome, suspended by concealed cast-iron girders, is a work of great engineering skill by Sir William Arrol, and the whole concept owes much to the 'Art Earl', as he was nicknamed. 'He has designed, I have planned', noted Lord Wemyss about Young.

And so in 1890 – a century since building work had begun on the new house at Gosford – Lord Wemyss and his family finally moved in. Yet the great house's heyday was to be little more than a golden Edwardian afternoon. The Art Earl died, aged 95 (and with a proud record of having sat in Parliament for more than 70 years) in 1914, and subsequently Gosford was occupied only intermittently. The 11th Earl, who preferred to base himself at the ravishing Cotswold manor house of Stanway, ended up running Gosford as an hotel. On the outbreak of the Second World War it was requisitioned by the military; in 1940 one huge room in Adam's centre block was gutted by fire.

After the war extensive dry rot was discovered and in 1948 most of the roof of the north wing was taken off. Yet, three years later and to his eternal credit, the present Lord Wemyss and his family returned to live at Gosford, where he adapted the south wing, which had escaped the fire and (almost) the dry rot, into a self-contained house of its own. A keen conservationist, who was to be an outstanding Chairman and President of the National Trust for Scotland for many years, Lord Wemyss managed to re-roof the burnt-out part of the middle block with the help of grants from the Historic Buildings Council for Scotland in the 1980s.

The inside, though, partly under the new roof, remains stark and uninhabitable. After the opulence of the Marble Hall and the richness of its works of art, it comes as a shock to be confronted with the bare, plasterless stone walls of the burnt-out Saloon next door. Curiously enough, this dramatic interior space, with its irresistible air of ruinous romance, has a haunting quality all of its own.

LEFT
Another view of the Gallery.

BELOW
The present Earl of Wemyss winding one of his beloved clocks at Gosford.

ABBOTSFORD

ROXBURGHSHIRE

BY THE narrow standards of an architectural purist, Abbotsford hardly qual-
ifies as a 'great' house. John Ruskin was one of many to sneer at its architecture;
even Queen Victoria herself found it 'rather gloomy'. Yet this extraordinarily
atmospheric shrine to Sir Walter Scott has an enduring appeal which
speaks out to the country-house visitor as no grander house ever does. So
potent is Sir Walter's personality that you feel that he might, at any moment,
pop his dome-like head round the door.

Sometimes one is even inclined to think that Scott actually invented
Scotland. Certainly no one did more to re-invent Scottish traditions after
the crushing of Scots pride at the Battle of Culloden. What the late Colin
McWilliam nicely described as 'the medievalistic gallimaufry of Abbotsford'
is a delightful distillation of this cultural conjuring trick. To Scott himself
it was an earthly paradise. 'I have seen much', he used to say, 'but nothing like my ain house.'

A younger son of an Edinburgh solicitor, Walter, lamed for life as a tod-
dler, was born in 1771 and spent his early years in the Borders, on his
grandfather's farm, before being educated in the New Town. His love of the
Border country never left him; the boy thrilled to stories about his ancestors such as Walter 'Beardie' Scott who was 'out' in the 1715 Jacobite Rising
and vowed never to shave until the Stuarts were restored to the throne.
As a young lawyer, serving as Sheriff-Depute of Selkirkshire, he would record
all the local traditions and ballads he heard on his peregrinations.

When published, these ballads proved commercially successful and
Scott went on to make a fortune with his own poems, such as *The Lay of
the Last Minstrel*. With the royalties Scott was able to satisfy his modest ambition to become a Tweedside laird on a minor scale. In 1811 he bought a

PRECEDING PAGES
The writer's Study – as if the great man had just popped out for a moment.

LEFT
Silhouette of Sir Walter at work.

RIGHT
The drawing room in the family wing.

farmstead called Cartleyhall on the south bank of the Tweed. Because the land had once belonged to Melrose Abbey, and there was a ford over the river by the house, Scott decided to rename the property Abbotsford.

He slightly extended the rather basic farmhouse, where he installed his growing family, and started writing novels. They were hugely profitable. A vast audience, hungry for romance about 'Olden Times', lapped up the *Waverley* novels in unprecedented quantities. Tales of Border life and High-land adventure flowed from Scott's fluent pen. Suddenly the best-selling novelist found himself rich enough to expand his estate and enlarge his house.

A wing was added in 1818 and four years later Sir Walter (as he had become in 1820 upon his creation as a Baronet) was in a position to pull down the old farmhouse and build a new country house. William Atkinson, of Scone Palace (see pages 72–81), was engaged as architect, with Edward Blore, an illustrator of books on Gothic whom Scott had discovered, contributing 'authentic' details.

With its battlemented tower, crow-stepped gables, conical turrets and strips of machicolation, all prefaced by castellated gateway and portcullis, Abbotsford could be described as being among the precursors of the style that was to become known as 'Scotch Baronial'. In many ways, it is unde-niably absurd. As Mark Girouard has pointed out, from the outside it 'looks rather more like a toy house than a real one'. The big 19th-century windows filled with plate glass hardly harmonize with the old-style towers and gables.

Once inside, though, any Sassenach sniggers are swiftly swallowed. With its moulded ceilings and dark polished panelling and Sir Walter's magpie collections of curios, Abbotsford buzzes with vitality. This is no faked-up sham but the heartfelt expression of a warm and potent imagination.

The Entrance Hall, for instance, contains oak panelling from the Auld Kirk at Dunfermline, bloodthirsty arms and armour of every date, a model of Robert the Bruce's skull, a stone fireplace copied from the cloisters of Melrose Abbey, relics of the Battle of Waterloo, an elk's head, a riot of heraldry – and so mind-bogglingly on. Yet somehow it all hangs together, like an intensely personal mosaic.

Scott's powerful personality projects itself down the centuries and pervades the house. Among the mementoes on view are the last clothes he wore – a grey beaver hat, a black cutaway coat and plaid trousers. You feel his presence most strongly in the book-galleried study, with his small writing desk made of wood supposedly from the ships of the Spanish Armada.

PRECEDING PAGES
Sir Walter's 'Baronial' hall, awash with armour.

BELOW
Corner full of curios.

In the Library, Scott, as portrayed in marble by Sir Francis Chantrey, holds pride of place. One of the books that most influenced him, an early 18th-century *Life of Rob Roy* lies open in a showcase alongside such cherished objects as Rob Roy's purse and a lock of Bonnie Prince Charlie's hair. A measure of the respect and affection which Sir Walter Scott inspired is shown by the presents on display, including the desk and set of chairs from King George IV in the Drawing Room. On meeting the novelist during his emotional visit to Scotland in 1822, the King (attired in flesh-coloured tights under his kilt) exclaimed: 'Sir Walter Scott! The man in Scotland I most wish to see!' The King's visit, which Scott himself largely stage-managed, was the zenith of the novelist's career.

Four years later came the nadir. The printing firm of Ballantyne, in which he was a sleeping partner, collapsed with spectacular debts, brought about by an unwise involvement with a London publisher. Scott, at the age of 55 and having only completed the rebuilding of his beloved Abbotsford a couple of years before, found himself faced with liabilities of £116,000 (several millions in today's money). He could have avoided them by going bankrupt, but he was far too honourable a man to escape what he saw as his responsibility. Instead he buckled down to grinding out the millions of words that were to pay off all the debts – and, doubtless, to destroy his health.

Yet the mood at Abbotsford is far from gloomy for Scott was a warm, lovable man, never happier than when working alongside his foresters in the woods or walking his devoted dogs. Canine characters enliven the picture collection at Abbotsford, whether Percy the greyhound as depicted by Sir Henry Raeburn or Ginger the terrier by Sir Edwin Landseer.

Sir Walter's famous last words to his son-in-law and biographer, J.G. Lockhart, are one of the most attractive aspects of the Scott tradition. 'My dear', he said, 'be a good man. Be virtuous, be religious, be a good man. Nothing else will give you any comfort when you come to lie here.' As the Laird lay dying in what is now the Dining Room at Abbotsford, Lockhart observed: 'It was so quiet a day that the sound he best loved, the gentle ripple of the Tweed over its pebbles, was distinctly audible as we knelt around his bed.'

Abbotsford had already become a place of pilgrimage before Sir Walter's death in 1832 and now it was opened regularly to the public. The volume of visitors proved so strong that in the 1850s J.R. Hope-Scott, QC, who married the eventual heiress of Abbotsford, Charlotte Lockhart (J.G's daughter), built a new family wing on to one side of the house. This wing, which contains a simple chapel, remains the home of Sir Walter's present-day descendant and the châtelaine of Abbotsford, Dame

LEFT
Sir Walter's 'Baronial' vision: the east elevation from the walled garden.

BELOW
A stone dog guards the private entrance to the family wing.

BOTTOM
Liveried firebuckets.

Jean Maxwell Scott, daughter of the late Major-General Sir Walter Maxwell-Scott, 1st and last Bt (Charlotte Lockhart's grandson). Together with her late sister, Patricia, Dame Jean has upheld Abbotsford's historic, friendly and hospitable tradition. Sir Walter's spirit lives on.

BOWHILL

SELKIRK

'WHEN summer smiled on sweet Bowhill', sang Sir Walter Scott in *The Lay of the Last Minstrel*, 'And July's eve, with balmy breath,/Watch the bluebells on Newark Heath...' The Laird of Abbotsford (see pages 186–95), who was proud of his kinship with the great Border dynasty of Scott of Buccleuch, plays a significant role in the story of Bowhill. He had the aged Last Minstrel recite his Lay at Newark Castle, one of the Scott strongholds (now a ruin) a couple of miles up the River Yarrow from the present Bowhill House, which is full of associations with the Border balladeer.

A close friend of the 4th Duke of Buccleuch, who shared his romantic passion for Border life, Sir Walter dedicated *The Lay of the Last Minstrel* to his wife ('my lovely chieftainess', as Scott described her). The manuscript of *The Lay* is now to be found in the Study at Bowhill, alongside the author's plaid and other relics. The room is dominated by Sir Henry Raeburn's celebrated portrait of Sir Walter with his faithful dog Camp at his feet.

As at the Buccleuchs' other seat of Drumlanrig (see pages 28–37), Sir Walter also took a close interest in the building improvements at Bowhill. Both the 4th and 5th Dukes benefited from his advice as the plain box-like early 18th-century house was transformed in the 19th century into first a Classical villa (to the designs of William Atkinson, also the architect of Abbotsford) and then into a Victorian pile (under the supervision of William Burn, who at the outset urged Sir Walter 'to promote my interest with the [5th] Duke').

The early 18th-century 'box' had been built by the Murray family, who had acquired the property from the Scotts in the 1690s. This, though, was merely an interregnum as Bowhill was in traditional Scott territory, and in 1745 the 2nd Duke of Buccleuch bought it back as an estate for his younger

PRECEDING PAGES
The Library, which is
the principal living room
of the present Duke and
Duchess of Buccleuch
when they are in
residence and which is
not part of the public
tour. It has been little
changed since 1814,
save for the installation
of the white marble
chimneypiece from
Dalkeith in 1948. The
'A' monogram indicates
that it was made (in
1705) for the Scott
heiress, the Duke of
Monmouth's widow,
Anne Duchess of
Buccleuch – whose
portrait by William
Wissing surmounts the
overmantel.

LEFT
The Upper Gallery of
the Gallery Hall, or
'Sallon', with its set
of Mortlake tapestries
(1670) of *The Triumph
of Julius Caesar* based
on Andrea Mantegna's
cartoons at Hampton
Court.

son. As things turned out, Bowhill's future role as a subsidiary family seat
was short-lived and it found itself promoted to higher billing. Lord Charles
Scott, the second surviving son of the 2nd Duke of Buccleuch, for whom
the property was intended, only survived a couple of years after its purchase
and, following the deaths of his elder brother and their father shortly
afterwards, Bowhill passed to Lord Charles's young nephew, the 3rd
Duke of Buccleuch.

The 3rd Duke – who married Lady Elizabeth Montagu, eventual heiress
of the Duke of Montagu – carried out some planting on the Bowhill
estate. A one-time pupil of the economist Adam Smith, author of *The Wealth*

The Drawing Room, created in 1831 when two rooms, one of them the original front hall on the south, were thrown together. The crimson wallcoverings date from the room's conversion. To the right is Sir Joshua Reynolds's portrait of the Montagu heiress, Elizabeth, who married the 3rd Duke of Buccleuch, together with her daughter, Lady Mary Scott.

of Nations, the 3rd Duke was an enlightened and progressive landowner with a dedication to dynamic and efficient land management that has remained the hallmark of the Bowhill estate to this day.

The 3rd Duke does not seem to have lived in the old house at Bowhill but his son, the future 4th Duke, began using it as an occasional summer house in the early years of the 19th century. Then, on succeeding to the Dukedom in 1812, he commissioned William Atkinson to add what amounted to a complete new Classical villa (including a central Saloon) to the south side of the existing house.

The remodelling appears to have been completed by 1814, though it was soon apparent that the new house was not big enough. Atkinson was duly asked to design flanking wings. First came the east wing, containing the Dining Room, and then, in 1819, the west. 'My prodigious undertaking of building a west wing to be added to the body of Bowhill is already

ABOVE
The Dining Room, added to the east of the house by William Atkinson in 1814/15 for the 4th Duke of Buccleuch. To the right of the fireplace is *The Pink Boy* by Sir Joshua Reynolds. To the left is Reynolds's exceptionally charming portrait of Lady Caroline Scott, muffled up as 'Winter'. On the far wall, to the right, is Canaletto's masterly study of Whitehall.

begun', the 4th Duke wrote in what was to be his last letter to Sir Walter Scott in February 1819.

His son Walter Francis, the 5th Duke, brought in William Burn from 1831 onwards to enlarge Bowhill. The main entrance was moved round to the north side, thereby making the south front private, and within the house the staircase was moved to the west, the Saloon was enlarged by taking in the cross corridor and the Drawing Room was extended by taking in Atkinson's entrance hall and porch.

Burn was to work off and on at Bowhill for nearly 40 years. Even after his death in 1870 the work was carried on by his nephew J. MacVicar Anderson, who was responsible for the Chapel, Billiard Room and Smoking Room. The result is that Bowhill grew and grew into a vast rambling house. Joined, as it is, to the stables, the whole frontage forms a continuous unit of 437 feet.

Yet, for all the improving Victorian zeal of the 5th Duke and his architects, they never lost sight of the fact that Bowhill is essentially a Georgian house. As John Cornforth has pointed out, Burn 'had to accept the extreme

RIGHT
'General Monk's bed' from a room at Dalkeith Palace which Monk used when planning the Restoration of the monarchy after Cromwell.

restraint of Atkinson's classicism' – on the outside, at least; within he was able to be more eclectic in the decoration.

No one could argue much of a case for Bowhill's architectural merits. On a grey day the exterior can look distinctly austere. However, its glorious setting (enhanced in the 19th century by the talents of the landscape designer and watercolourist William Sawrey Gilpin), homely atmosphere (notwithstanding its size) and, above all, its fabulous collections of treasures combine to give Bowhill a special place among the great houses of Scotland.

The sheer quality of the contents impresses visitors the moment they enter the towering Sallon, or Gallery Hall as it is now more familiarly known. Up above Burn's balustrade, the eye takes in three Mortlake tapestries. Below hang splendid portraits by Sir Peter Lely and Sir Anthony Van Dyck. Here, too, is a sumptuous feast of French furniture and an exquisite Louis XIV mirror of ebony, tortoiseshell and ormolu, given by King Charles II to his son, the Duke of Monmouth.

The Monmouth Room is dedicated to the Duke's memory and contains such relics as his magnificent saddle and the white linen shirt in which he was executed in 1685 after the crushing of his Rebellion. The Room also includes a series of topographical views by the 18th-century landscapist George Barret. The finest topographical work at Bowhill, though, is, of course, Canaletto's luminous view of Whitehall, which hangs harmoniously with a dazzling display of family portraits in the Dining Room. Reynolds's charming study of the muffled Lady Caroline Scott (sister of the 4th Duke) as 'Winter' would come high on many people's list of their favourite pictures.

It is tempting to drool on about the marvellous treasures of Bowhill, which have been greatly enhanced this century since the closure of two of the Buccleuchs' other palaces, Montagu House in London and Dalkeith, near Edinburgh (now let to an American university). Yet, as the present Duke of Buccleuch points out, Bowhill is 'much more than a great family home, with a unique art collection in the setting with which it is historically associated.' It is, he stresses, the focal point of the estate.

Successive Dukes of Buccleuch have traditionally regarded the care and productivity of the land, together with the well-being of everyone upon it, as a primary duty. The present Duke has dedicated his considerable energies to 'demonstrating that it is on a private agricultural estate, such as this, that the conflict of interests between farming, forestry, conservation, amenity and sport can most successfully be reconciled to the local and national advantage.' Besides opening the house every July, the Duke also regularly opens part of the estate as a 'Country Park', complete with prize-winning educational facilities, adventure playground and nature trails along the lochs and rivers of this Border paradise.

MOUNT STUART

ISLE OF BUTE

A VISIT to Mount Stuart on the still pleasingly unspoilt Isle of Bute tends to leave one deprived of the power of speech. Like an old hippy, one finds oneself mouthing such inanities as, 'That's something else, man, far out...'. Such New Age argot may perhaps, be explained by the dazzling array of astrological mumbo-jumbo incorporated into the design of this amazing Gothic extravaganza built for the 3rd Marquess of Bute, one of the richest and certainly one of the most unusual aristocrats of the late 19th century.

The mystical Marquess was born – as we can tell from the elaborate astrological ceiling of his bedroom, which depicts the position of the planets at the time of his nativity – on September 12, 1847, at Mount Stuart, then a rather barrack-like Georgian box (originally designed by Alexander McGill in 1716 and remodelled by George Paterson in 1780). His father, the 2nd Marquess of Bute, who had secured the family fortune by transforming Cardiff, on his Welsh estates, into a major port, died only six months later. The infant Marquess was to enjoy a great inheritance.

His father descended from the Royal House of Stuart, a line long seated at Rothesay Castle on the Isle of Bute, of which the head of the family was Hereditary Keeper. The 2nd Marquess also inherited the Earldom of Dumfries from his maternal grandfather and accordingly prefixed his surname with Crichton. The most prominent member of the family had been the 3rd Earl of Bute, King George III's much-maligned Prime Minister. Many of the non-Victorian contents at Mount Stuart today came from the Prime Minister Bute's splendid collections of paintings and furniture formerly housed at his Bedfordshire seat of Luton Hoo, which was rebuilt for him by his fellow Scot, Robert Adam.

PRECEDING PAGES
'Was there ever such a
hall for hide-and-seek?'
asked the 3rd Marquess
of Bute's friend and
biographer, Abbot Sir
David Hunter Blair, 5th
Bt. Less prosaically he
described this astonishing
interior as a 'vast hall
gleaming with light'.

LEFT
View up to the stained
glass above the third-
floor gallery of the
Marble Hall.

RIGHT
The vaulted Marble
Staircase. The decorative
paintings in the spandrels
of the arches (illustrating
the Days of Creation)
and the heraldic glass
in the windows were
executed by H.W.
Lonsdale.

The 3rd Marquess's own passion for art and architecture knew no
bounds. Not for nothing is the ceiling of the Horoscope Room at Mount
Stuart adorned with a frieze of miniature castles. Altogether he is reck-
oned to have sponsored some 60 building projects and to have acted as
patron to a dozen architects, most famously the eccentric genius 'Billy'
Burges, with whom he rebuilt much of Cardiff Castle.

On coming of age in 1868 the 3rd Marquess caused a sensation by
being received into the Roman Catholic Church. Benjamin Disraeli was
inspired by Lord Bute's conversion to write his novel *Lothair*. The Marquess
took to wearing a cloak like a monk's habit, studied Hebrew in order to

translate the Roman Breviary and steeped himself in astrology, the occult and the lives of little-known Scottish saints.

Initially, Lord Bute's improvements at Mount Stuart on coming into his heritage were on a minor scale. Burges designed a new chapel for the old house, which also acquired a new entrance hall, and the animal-loving Marquess introduced beavers and wallabies into the woods. Then, in 1877, the central block of the 18th-century house was gutted by fire.

This was the opportunity that Lord Bute had been waiting for. He commissioned the Edinburgh-born medievalist Robert Rowand Anderson (later

ABOVE
The Marble Hall arcade and *The Lord of the Hunt* tapestry, designed by William Skeoch Cumming – the first to be woven at the Dovecot Studio, established in Edinburgh by the 4th Marquess of Bute.

Sir Robert and best known for his Scottish National Portrait Gallery), who had studied under the great Goth, Sir Gilbert Scott. 'Anderson's plans are exceedingly nice', wrote Lord Bute to his wife, the former Gwendolen Fitzalan-Howard (eldest daugher of the 1st Lord Howard of Glossop), in the autumn of 1879. 'The house seems to bid fair to be a splendid palace'.

No expense was to be spared. 'I have not made up my mind', remarked Lord Bute to his friend Sir Herbert Maxwell as they studied a model of the new Mount Stuart complete with a great central hall to be surrounded by pillars, 'whether these pillars shall be marble or granite.'

In the event, marbles were chosen, 'the rarest', as Lord Bute's friend and biographer, Abbot Sir David Hunter Blair, 5th Bt, a Benedictine monk, put it: '*pavonozetto*, emperor's red, *cipollino* columns crowned with capitals of purest white and arches of grey Sicilian.' The Marble Hall, to which they give their name, is reminiscent of a stupendous cathedral, lit by rich stained-glass which projects bursts of colour on to the stonework. The sky-like ceiling, decorated by Charles Campbell, who worked with Burges at Cardiff, is a kaleidoscope of glinting, glass stars. By contrast with the exotic splendour of the Marble Hall, the Chapel is a vision of white purity, relieved only by the blood-red rays pouring in from the crimson stained glass.

The building work, though, took rather too long even for Lord Bute's delight in detail ('But why should I hurry over what is my chief pleasure?' he once protested). Anderson was eventually replaced, at the fitting-out stage of the interior, by Burges's assistant, William Frame, whose fondness for the bottle hardly hastened progress. 'Frame being drunk again',

BELOW LEFT
The astrological ceiling of the Horoscope Room, showing the position of the planets at the time of the 3rd Marquess of Bute's birth on September 12, 1847.

BELOW RIGHT
The elaborate heraldic ceiling – a literal family tree – in the Drawing Room.

LEFT
The Horoscope Room, the bedroom of
the 3rd Marquess of Bute, leading to
his observatory (now a conservatory).

ABOVE
The Drawing Room, divided by screens
of marble columns. The ceiling was
coloured in 1899.

noted Lord Bute in his diary in 1890, 'had to dismiss him.' Anderson
was reinstated and building work resumed at a snail's pace. The Chapel was
only begun in 1896, the eaves gallery around the west front in 1899.

Operations came to an abrupt halt the next year when Lord Bute
died of a stroke, aged 53 (his heart was later buried on the Mount of Olives).
His widow, though, later proceeded with the finishing-off of such interiors as the Libraries and the swimming pool – a bizarre exercise in subterranean
Gothic reminiscent of *The Phantom of the Opera*.

With the dawn of a new century there was a violent reaction against
the perceived 'hideousness' of Victorian Gothic and in 1920 the 4th
Marquess of Bute, the first chairman of the Scottish National Buildings
Record, went so far as to offer Mount Stuart for sale 'conditional to its complete demolition and removal by the Purchaser.... Suitable for re-erection as
an Hotel, Hydro, Restaurant, Casino, Public Building, Etc.'

Fortunately for posterity there were no takers. Sixty years on, the 6th Marquess of Bute, an inspirational chairman of both the National Trust for Scotland and the Historic Buildings Council for Scotland, nobly embarked, together with his second wife, Jennifer, and the conservation architect Stewart Tod, on a full-scale repair of the fabric and restoration of the interiors. The Marble Hall was cleaned, its glass stars refitted, the stained-glass windows releaded, the mullions regilded. The Dining Room was rehung with a Crace wallpaper; the overmantel by John Adam in the Red Drawing Room triumphantly restored. The 3rd Marquess's observatory became a conservatory; the Horoscope Room was brilliantly recreated. Outside, the roof was completely overhauled, the stonework repointed. A new 'family entrance', with carvings by Dick Reid, was also created on the west side of the house.

Today the Mount Stuart Trust opens the house and gardens 'as a centre for the wider enjoyment and better understanding of their unique historical, architectural, cultural and botanical features.' What the late Marquess's elder son and heir, the former racing driver Johnny Dumfries (joint winner of Le Mans in 1988), nicely described in a tribute to his father as Mount Stuart's 'outrageous beauty' has been stylishly preserved for future generations. And Johnny Bute is carrying on his father's good work with infectious enthusiasm. Recent improvements have included Tom Errington's murals of Celtic Saints in the Chapel, the restoration of the family bedroom and its friezes of St Margaret, as well as a new visitor centre.

MANDERSTON

BERWICKSHIRE

AT MANDERSTON in the Borders we arrive in the Edwardian era when country-house comfort and opulence had attained its apogee. This amazing custom-built dream world of sybaritic luxury has rightly been called the swansong of the great Classical house. Although some purists may find the exterior a touch ponderous, notwithstanding the razor-sharp masonry, the 'Adam Revival' interiors are of breathtaking quality. The attention to detail throughout the house and its policies is absolutely tip-top; the materials and craftsmanship are of a standard that can only be described as unique – in the case of the Silver Staircase literally so, for it is the only one of its kind in the world.

This enviable Edwardian paradise was created for Sir James Miller, 2nd Bt, a famous figure on the Turf known as 'Lucky Jim', by the architect John Kinross. Lucky Jim's father, William, who had made a fortune trading hemp and herring with the Russians, bought the estate in 1860 on the death of his brother Richard, who had acquired it five years earlier. The property then consisted of a square late-Georgian box, originally built for a Mr Dalhousie Weatherstone in the 1790s, probably to the designs of Alexander Gilkie or John White.

William Miller, who was a Liberal MP rumoured never to have spoken in the House of Commons, aggrandized – or to be less polite, mucked about with – the old house in 1871 to the designs of an architect called John Simpson. A pillared entrance porch was added and extra servants' bedrooms installed under a bizarre new Frenchified roof.

Three years later William Miller was created a Baronet on the recommendation of William Gladstone, grateful for Miller's well-contrived political dinners. In the same year, 1874, his eldest son and namesake fatally

choked on a cherry stone at Eton and so Manderston passed to the second son, Lucky Jim. As *Vanity Fair* magazine pointed out in 1890, the new
Baronet, 'being a good fellow, one of the most wealthy commoners in
the country and a bachelor, he is a very eligible young man.' In the event,
he married Eveline Curzon, daughter of the 4th Lord Scarsdale and younger
sister of the great George Nathaniel Curzon, soon to be appointed Viceroy
of India. The splendid Curzon family seat of Kedleston in Derbyshire, Robert
Adam's masterpiece, obviously made a strong impression on Sir James Miller.
Here, surely, was a case of Lucky Jim showing his by then somewhat impoverished in-laws that anything they could do he could do better.

Before his marriage in 1893 Sir James had already begun improving
Manderston. New garden terraces and a horse-shoe stair were added to
the south front by Kinross in 1890. In the spirit of the age, sport took a high
priority for Lucky Jim, who was an excellent shot as well as a racehorse owner.
In 1895 Kinross built a gamekeeper's cottage, kennels and a home farm
on the estate, plus a stable block in the Classical manner which, as *Horse and*

PRECEDING PAGES
View through the Hall,
with organ in ante-room at
foot of stairs.

RIGHT
The only Silver Staircase in
the world. In Manderston's
Edwardian heyday it would
take three men three weeks
to dismantle, polish and
put it back together. It was
restored in 1980.

BELOW
The Hall: shades of
Kedleston, the home of
Sir James Miller's Curzon
in-laws.

Hound magazine has remarked, 'probably boasts the finest stabling in all the world'.

If one thinks the horses were pampered at Manderston, the cows visiting the Marble Dairy around a delightful cloister must have assumed sacred status. Inside the milkhouse, the boss in the centre of the rib-vaulted roof featured a milkmaid at work. Manderston's own boss, though, Sir James Miller, spotted that the girl was sitting on the wrong side of the cow; the half-ton stone ornament had to be taken down and recarved. Perfectionism was the order of the day; cost did not count.

From 1901 Kinross created a new north front to the main house with an imposing Ionic portico. If the outside was a little austere, in keeping with Classical restraint, the inside was an exuberant 'Adam' fantasy awash with apses, domes, covings and columns. It is fun to spot the allusions to Kedleston – such as the chimneypiece in the spacious central Hall; the ceiling in the Ballroom, cribbed from the dining room at Kedleston; and the display of Derbyshire Bluejohn in the house's own Dining Room.

The Ballroom, which opens dramatically from the Drawing Room, conjures up a delicious floating sensation. It is decorated in Lucky Jim's racing colours of primrose and white, which were best known for carrying

his owner-bred horse Rock Sand to the Turf's 'Triple Crown' (the Two Thousand Guineas, Derby and St Leger) in 1903. Done up as it was in the era of the *Entente Cordiale*, the French influence is strong at Manderston. The Silver Staircase (brilliantly restored in 1980 after not being cleaned for nearly 70 years) was inspired by the *Petit Trianon*. Even in the Marble Dairy one is reminded of Marie Antoinette, though the panelled room where Lady Miller took tea above is housed in a tower built to look like a Border Keep that could hardly be more Scottish.

In the handsomely stuccoed Dining Room, the last interior to be completed when the house was finished in 1905, one's thoughts turn from the ceiling carved in high relief to fantasies about Edwardian breakfasts. That the pleasures of the table were well organized in this establishment is nicely illustrated by the six separate white-tiled larders downstairs: one each for ice, pastry, raw meat, cooked meat, game and fish (complete with fountain) – an arrangement to satisfy the fussiest Brussels bureaucrat.

Indeed the 'downstairs' aspect of Manderston is in some ways even more evocative of the Edwardian age than the 'upstairs'. No detail was too insignificant in the quest for supreme comfort. Even the kitchens were decorated by Kinross, the architect. In Manderston's heyday, 46 servants (22 inside, 24 out) were required to keep the household ticking over smoothly. Alas, that heyday was all too brief, for Sir James Miller's luck ran out in 1906, when he died, childless, aged 41, only a few months after his dream house was finished.

The Baronetcy expired a dozen years later with the death of Sir James's youngest brother, but Sir James's widow lived on at Manderston until the 1930s when the estate was inherited by Major Hugh Bailie (son of Lucky Jim's elder sister, Amy). The Major was a keen horticulturist and after the Second World War planted an extensive and colourful woodland garden with a specialist collection of rhododendrons and azaleas, which are a magnificent attraction in their own right.

Before Major Bailie died in 1978 he made over Manderston to his grandson, Adrian Palmer (now the 4th Lord Palmer), elder son of the Major's elder daughter, Lorna, the wife of Col Sir Gordon Palmer. Sir Gordon, who was chairman of the celebrated Reading biscuit firm of Huntley & Palmer (hence the amusing exhibition of biscuit tins in the basement), played a significant role in securing Manderston's future by helping to persuade the authorities that the property should be granted Heritage exemption from capital taxation.

Adrian Palmer and his new bride, Cornelia Wadham (sister of the actor Julian Wadham), threw themselves energetically into opening Manderston to the public and making the house pay its way through private and

PRECEDING PAGES
The Drawing Room, opening into the Ballroom.

corporate hospitality, film and television location work and all the other necessities of modern country-house life. The Palmers, who have lovingly restored the palatial house and its 56 acres of gardens, represent at its best the practical new generation of historic house owners.

ARDKINGLAS

ARGYLL

THE EDWARDIAN plutocrats were surely dream patrons for architects. At Ardkinglas on Loch Fyne, as at Manderston (see pages 218–27), the building brief was, so to speak, 'nothing but the best and hang the expense'. No wonder the great, if under-valued, architect Robert Lorimer – later Sir Robert and sometimes called 'the Scots Lutyens' – regarded this as his favourite commission. His client Sir Andrew Noble, 1st Bt, the armaments pioneer (and brother-in-law of Isambard Brunel junior), gave him a free hand to design the entire house down to the minutest detail. The only *caveat*, as communicated by Sir Andrew's energetic spinster daughter, Lilias ('Lily'), was to proceed with all haste as the old boy was in his mid-seventies when Lorimer began work in 1906.

Not the least remarkable thing about this lovable, romantic house, which blends so harmoniously with its dramatic Highland landscape, is that it was built merely as a shooting lodge, a holiday home, for Sir Andrew. As chairman of Armstrong's, the armament company, this expatriate Scot was based south of the border, in Northumberland, where he rented such houses as Jesmond Dene (designed by Norman Shaw). Noble was knighted and then, in 1902, created a Baronet in recognition of his important experiments in gunnery and explosives.

'Shooting lodge' or not, one wonders whether Sir Andrew might have had it in mind to show his old boss, Lord Armstrong, who had commissioned Norman Shaw to turn his modest weekend retreat of Cragside into a cavernous pile, that he too could make something of a splash. Yet, though adorned with Baronial flourishes, Lorimer's sympathetic plan for Ardkinglas harked back to the vernacular architecture of late 17th-century Scotland. The local stone used was a granite of greenish hue patched with gold. The dressed quoins are of a cool, dark cream-coloured stone from Dullatur; the delightfully modelled roofs are covered with Caithness slate now weathered, as Charles Maclean has nicely observed, to 'the colour of malt whisky'.

Lorimer envisaged a building that would epitomize, in its pale mass, the rhythms of its setting against the dark, majestic mountains. As such, Ardkinglas can be seen, to quote the architect's biographer, Christopher Hussey, as 'a remarkable instance of expressionist design'. Lorimer's genius was to subordinate the intellectual processes of design to what Hussey calls 'his sensuous intuitions'.

All this aesthetic theorizing was a luxury that could be indulged in later. For the moment, the rush was on to get the house built. Sir Andrew Noble had bought the estate in 1905 from, according to a family memoir, 'the trustees of the estate of two Callander brothers who suffered from intermittent fits of lunacy'. The attraction of the place was that Sir

PRECEDING PAGES
What could be more agreeable? A summer luncheon laid out in the Loggia.

RIGHT
A corner of the Saloon, with its great windows facing Loch Fyne.

BELOW
The entrance front of the lovably Scots creation of Sir Robert Lorimer, which blends so harmoniously with the landscape.

Andrew's Scots-Canadian wife, Margery, was a Campbell and Ardkinglas was very much Campbell country, being situated across Loch Fyne from Inveraray (see pages 160–69).

In 1396 Sir Colin Campbell, the then *Mac Calein Mor*, granted the estate of Ardkinglas to a younger son, Caileen Oig, 'in all its righteous heaths and marches, or as long as woods shall grow and waters flow'. His descendants had the characteristic Highland history, full of murder, magic, family feuds, witches and warlocks. The old castle at Ardkinglas is recorded as undergoing repairs in 1586. According to an account by Sir John Sinclair it had three separate towers and a stout wall, gatehouse, flanking turrets and a defending tower. The Georgian house that replaced it was already half-derelict by the time Dorothy Wordsworth, the poet's sister, arrived in 1822 to wander through the estate and admire the woods – still one of Ardkinglas's most beautiful features and now boasting some of the finest specimen

ABOVE
The Saloon, or Drawing Room, dominated by its massive fireplace, with a lintel carved from a single slab of granite weighing more than five tons.

RIGHT
One of the first country houses to have electricity, Ardkinglas has a series of stylish light fixtures designed by Lorimer to complement his ceilings.

conifers in Britain, as well as an outstanding collection of rhododendrons. (The woodland gardens are open to the public.)

ABOVE LEFT
All modern conveniences at Ardkinglas, including this Lorimer-designed shower-cage.

To enable Ardkinglas Mark III to be built, Lorimer had to arrange the construction of a pier on to Loch Fyne for all the building materials, apart from the local stone for the walls, had to be shipped in from afar. In these circumstances it is all the more remarkable that the new house was actually finished within little more than 18 months.

ABOVE RIGHT
The tiled kitchen and scullery, still in use.

As Christopher Hussey noted, the impression one takes from Ardkinglas is that 'it is in every way entirely practical, and that the historical flavour of the building has not been won at the cost of any single feature of convenience or modern comfort'. The rooms are grouped under a compact open courtyard. On the ground floor Lorimer furnished Sir Andrew with an oval Study of great charm, and a Smoking-cum-Billiards room. A stately stone staircase leads up to the Morning Room and the house's principal interior, the Saloon, with its windows overlooking Loch Fyne.

This most agreeable oak-panelled room, 45 feet by 22 feet, is dominated by a massive fireplace, which has a lintel carved from a single slab

of granite weighing more than five tons. The ceiling is adorned with one of Lorimer's robust 17th-century-style exercises in garlanded plasterwork. The central panel contains an unexpected painting of Apollo by Roger Fry, the Bloomsbury artist, critic and founder of the Omega Workshop. For all his traditionalist leanings, Lorimer had links with the Arts & Crafts movement and was influenced by *Art Nouveau*. A close study of the interior of Ardkinglas reveals an enchantingly original series of design details – whether light fixtures, door handles or keyhole flaps.

The principal bedrooms were also situated on the first floor as well as the Dining Room and the spacious Loggia, looking out to the loch. Most of the bedrooms up on the second floor have pretty plastered and vaulted ceilings. The tower at the top of the house affords glorious views down Loch Fyne to Dunderave and beyond to Inveraray.

The halcyon days of Edwardian sporting holidays at Ardkinglas came to an end in 1915 when Sir Andrew Noble died – 'called over', as a chronicler described it, by the roaring of stags in Glen Kinglas. Subsequently the house ceased to be just a summer retreat; and indeed today it is the centre of a flourishing estate run with commendable gusto and enterprise by John Noble, Sir Andrew's great-grandson.

This refreshingly unstuffy bachelor Laird has ingeniously turned Ardkinglas into a hive of local industry without spoiling its essentially relaxed, comfortable atmosphere. The flagship concern is Loch Fyne Oysters, the now world-famous seafood company which Johnny Noble founded together with Andrew Lane, a local fish farmer in 1978. Their hunch that the clear, unpolluted waters of Loch Fyne, warmed by the Gulf Stream, would prove ideal for growing oysters and other shellfish has been triumphantly vindicated. Today fresh oysters, langoustines, *Bradan Orach* (golden smoked salmon) and other delicacies, not forgetting the legendary Loch Fyne kippers, are sent all over the globe.

Inspired by the tradition of the old 'howfs' (cellars) in 18th-century Edinburgh, Johnny Noble has also opened a popular Oyster Bar across the loch from Ardkinglas in a converted farm building at Cairndow, where delicious seafood is served in simple surroundings for one and all to enjoy. Further Loch Fyne Oyster Bars have also been opened in England.

The upshot of all this activity is that, as Johnny Noble points out, the Ardkinglas estate now 'provides as many if not more jobs than it did in Andrew Noble's time'. Life, in short, still goes on in the great houses of Scotland – and there could be no friendlier or more romantic place at which to end our grand tour than Ardkinglas, an amalgam of Scots vernacular architecture through the ages subtly combined with the expansive comfort of *la belle époque*.

ADDRESSES AND CONTACT DETAILS

ALMOST ALL the 25 houses featured in this book are open regularly to the public – with the exceptions of Ardkinglas and Kinross, where only the gardens are open, and Newhailes, which is currently under restoration. Full details of the facilities, opening times, price of admission, etc., can be found in the annual directory, *Hudson's Historic Houses and Gardens.* Below are given the addresses, Ordnance Survey map references and telephone numbers (where appropriate) of the houses (in alphabetical sequence) featured in the book for ease of reference. Callers from outside the United Kingdom should add 44 and omit the first 0.

ABBOTSFORD HOUSE
Melrose, Roxburghshire
TD6 9BQ
OS NT 508 343
Tel: 01896-752043

ARDKINGLAS
(Woodland Gardens only
open)
Cairndow, Argyll
PA26 8BH
OS NN 173 106
Tel: 01499-600261

ARNISTON HOUSE
Gorebridge, Midlothian
EH23 4RY
OS NT 326 595
Tel: 01875-830515

BLAIR CASTLE
Pitlochry, Perthshire
PH18 5TL
OS NN 880 660
Tel: 01796-481207

BOWHILL HOUSE
Bowhill, Selkirk
TD7 5ET
OS NT 426 278
Tel: 01750-22204

CAWDOR CASTLE
Nairn
IV12 5RD
OS NH 850 500
Tel: 01667-404 674

CULZEAN CASTLE
Maybole, Ayrshire
KA19 8LE
OS NS 240 100
Tel: 01655-884455

DALMENY HOUSE
South Queensferry, nr
Edinburgh
West Lothian
EH30 9TQ
OS NT 167 779
Tel: 0131-331 1888

DRUMLANRIG CASTLE
Thornhill, Dumfriesshire
DG3 4AQ
OS NX 851 992
Tel: 01848-330248

DUFF HOUSE
Banff
AB45 3SX
OS NT 691 634
Tel: 01261-818181

DUNROBIN CASTLE
Golspie, Sutherland
KW10 6SF
OS NC 850 010
Tel: 01408-633177

GLAMIS CASTLE
by Forfar, Angus
DD8 1RJ
OS NO 386 480
Tel: 01307-840393

GOSFORD HOUSE
Longniddry, East Lothian
EH32 0PX
OS NT 453 786
Tel: 01875-870201

HADDO HOUSE
Tarves, Ellon
Aberdeenshire
AB41 0ER
OS NT 868 348
Tel: 01651-851440

HOPETOUN HOUSE
South Queensferry, nr
Edinburgh
West Lothian
EH30 9SL
OS NT 089 790
Tel: 0131-331 2451

(THE) HOUSE OF DUN
Montrose, Angus
DD10 9LQ
OS NO 670 599
Tel: 01674-810264

INVERARAY CASTLE
Inveraray, Argyll
PA32 8XE
OS NN 100 090
Tel: 01499-302203

KINROSS HOUSE
(Gardens only open)
Kinross
KY13 8EU

MANDERSTON
Duns, Berwickshire
TD11 3PP
OS NT 810 544
Tel: 01361-883450

MELLERSTAIN HOUSE
Gordon, Berwickshire
TD3 6LG
OS NT 648 392
Tel: 01573-410225

MOUNT STUART
Isle of Bute
PA20 9LR
OS NS100 600
Tel: 01700-503877

SCONE PALACE
Perth
PH2 6BD
OS NO 114 266
Tel: 01738-552300

THIRLESTANE CASTLE
Lauder, Berwickshire
TD2 6RU
OS NT 540 473
Tel: 01578-722430

TRAQUAIR HOUSE
Innerleithen, Peeblesshire
EH44 6PW
OS NY 330 354
Tel: 01896-830323

SELECT BIBLIOGRAPHY

ADAM, Robert, and ADAM, James, *The Works in Architecture*, London, 1975 (reprint)

ADAM, William, *Vitruvius Scoticus*, Edinburgh, 1980 (reprint)

Apollo magazine: special issue on Dalmeny House, June, 1984

ASLET, Clive, *The Last Country Houses*, New Haven and London, 1982

BATEMAN, John, *The Great Land-owners of Britain and Ireland*, London, 1833 (4th edn)

BEARD, Geoffrey, *The Work of Robert Adam*, Edinburgh, 1978

BENCE-JONES, Mark, *The Catholic Families*, London, 1992

BENCE-JONES, Mark, and MONTGOMERY-MASSINGBERD, Hugh, *The British Aristocracy*, London, 1979

BILLINGS, R.W., *The Antiquities of Scotland*, Edinburgh, 1852 (4 vols)

BINNEY, Marcus, 'Gothic Revival', *The Times Magazine*, June 10, 1995

BOLTON, Arthur T., *The Architecture of Robert and James Adam*, London, 1922 (2 vols)

BURKE, Sir Bernard, *Burke's Peerage, Baronetage & Knightage*, London, 1826–1999 (106 editions)

— *Burke's Dormant and Extinct Peerages*, London, 1969 (reprint)

— *Burke's Landed Gentry*, London, 1833–1972 (18 editions)

— *A Visitation of the Seats and Arms of the Noblemen and Gentlemen of Great Britain and Ireland*, London, 1852–5 (4 vols)

CAMPBELL, Colen, *Vitruvius Britannicus*, London, 1715–25 (3 vols)

CANTLIE, Hugh, *Ancestral Castles of Scotland*, London, 1992

CAWDOR, 6th Earl, *Cawdor Castle*, Cawdor, 1992

G.E.C. and others (eds), *The Complete Peerage*, London, 1910–59 (13 vols); Gloucester, 1982 (microprint, 6 vols)

COLVIN, H.M., *A Biographical Dictionary of British Architects, 1600–1840*, London, 1978

CONNACHAN-HOLMES, John, *Country Houses of Scotland*, Isle of Colonsay, 1995

CORNFORTH, John, 'Bowhill, Selkirk', *Country Life*, June 5, 12, 19 and 26, 1975

— 'Duff House, Banffshire', *Country Life*, September 21, 1995

— 'The House of Dun, Angus', *Country Life*, November 10, 1986, and June 22, 1989

— 'Manderston, Berwickshire', *Country Life*, February 15 and 22 and March 1, 1979 and August 26, 1993

— 'Newhailes, East Lothian', *Country Life*, November 21 and 28, 1996

— 'Scone Palace, Perthshire', *Country Life*, August 11 and 18, 1988

COUNTRY LIFE: see Binney, Cornforth, Duncan, Girouard, Hall, Hunt, Pryke, Robinson and Rowan

DAICHES, David, *Sir Walter Scott*, London, 1971

Dictionary of National Biography

DOUGLAS, Sir Robert (ed), *Peerage of Scotland*, Edinburgh, 1813 (2nd edn, 2 vols)

DRUMMOND, Maldwin (ed), *John Bute*, Wilby, 1996

DUNBAR, John G., *The Historic Architecture of Scotland*, London, 1996

— *Sir William Bruce, 1630–1710*, Edinburgh, 1970

DUNCAN, Paul, 'Newhailes, East

Lothian', *Country Life*, January 29 and February 5, 1987

FEDDEN, Robin, and KENWORTHY-BROWNE, John, *The Country House Guide*, London, 1979 (with Scottish section by Colin McWilliam)

FENWICK, Hubert, *Architect Royal: The Life and Works of Sir William Bruce*, London, 1970

— *Scotland's Castles*, London, 1976

— *Scotland's Historic Buildings*, London, 1974

— *Scottish Baronial Houses*, London, 1986

FLEMING, John, *Scottish Country Houses and Gardens Open to the Public*, London, 1954

FORMAN, Sheila, *Scottish Country Houses and Castles*, Glasgow, 1967

GIFFORD, John, *The Buildings of Scotland: Highlands and Islands*, London, 1992

— *The Buildings of Scotland: Dumfries and Galloway*, London, 1996

GIROUARD, Mark, *Historic Houses of Britain*, London, 1979

— *The Victorian Country House*, New Haven and London, 1979

— 'Kinross House, Kinross-shire', *Country Life*, March 25 and April 1, 1965

GORDON, Archie, *A Wild Flight of Gordons*

GORDON, Sir Robert, *A Genealogical History of the Earldom of Sutherland*, Edinburgh, 1813

GOW, Ian, and CLIFFORD, Timothy, *Duff House*, Edinburgh, 1995

GREVILLE, Charles, *Journals of the Reign of Queen Victoria, 1837–1952*, London, 1885 (3 vols)

GRIERSON, Sir H.J.C. (ed), *Letters of Sir Walter Scott*, London, 1932–7 (12 vols)

HALL, Michael, 'Mount Stuart, Isle of Bute', *Country Life*, June 15, 1995

HARTLEY, Christopher, *Haddo House*, Edinburgh, 1989

— *The House of Dun*, Edinburgh, 1992

HILL, Oliver, *Scottish Castles of the 16th and 17th Centuries*, London, 1953

HUNT, John, 'Gosford, East Lothian', *Country Life*, October 12 and November 4, 1971

HUSSEY, Christopher, *The Work of Sir Robert Lorimer*, London, 1931

INNES-SMITH, Robert, *Glamis Castle*, Derby, 1993

JACKSON-STOPS, Gervase (ed), *Treasure Houses of Britain*, New Haven and London, 1985

JOHNSON, EDGAR, *Sir Walter Scott: The Great Unknown*, London, 1970

LEARMONT, David, and RIDDLE, Gordon, *Culzean Castle and Country Park*, Edinburgh, 1992

LEES-MILNE, James, *The Age of Adam*, London, 1947

LINDSAY, Ian G., and COSH, Mary, *Inveraray and the Dukes of Argyll*, Edinburgh, 1973

LOCKHART, John Gibson, *Life of Scott*, Edinburgh, 1837–8

MACAULAY, James, *The Classical Country House in Scotland, 1660–1800*, London, 1987

— *The Gothic Revival, 1745–1845*, Glasgow and London, 1975

MACAULAY, T.B., *History of England*, London, 1849–61 (5 vols)

MACGIBBON, David and ROSS, Thomas, *The Castellated and Domestic Architecture of Scotland*, Edinburgh, 1887–92 (5 vols)

MACLEAN, Charles and SYKES, Christopher Simon, *Scottish Country*, London, 1992

MACLEAN, Fitzroy, *A Concise History of Scotland*, London, 1970

McWILLIAM, Colin, *The Buildings of Scotland: Lothian*, London, 1978

MASTERS, Brian, *The Dukes*, London, 1980 (2nd edn)

MAXWELL-SCOTT, Maj-Gen Sir Walter, Bt, *Abbotsford*, Abbotsford

MAXWELL STUART, Flora, *Lady Nithsdale and the Jacobites*, Traquair, 1995

MONCREIFFE of that Ilk, Sir Iain, Bt, *The Highland Clans*, London and Exeter, 1988

— 'Heritage' (and 'Family Seats') articles in *The Field*, 1976–1987, and *The Daily Telegraph*, 1987–96

MONTGOMERY-MASSINGBERD, Hugh, (ed), *Lord of the Dance: A Moncreiffe Miscellany*, London, 1986

NEALE, J.P., *Views of the Seats of Noblemen and Gentlemen*, London, 1819

NICOLSON, Nigel, *Great Houses of Britain*, London, 1978

NOBLE, Sir Humphrey, Bt, *Life in Noble Houses*, 1969

PATTULLO, Nan, *Castles, Houses and Gardens of Scotland*, Edinburgh, 1967

PETZSCH, Helmut, *Architecture in Scotland*, London, 1971

PRENTICE, Robin (ed), *The National Trust for Scotland Guide*, London, 1981 (3rd edn)

PRYKE, Sebastian, 'Hopetoun House, West Lothian', *Country Life*, August 10, 1995

RICHARDSON, Sir Albert, *Robert Mylne, Architect and Engineer, 1782–1811*, London, 1955

ROBINSON, John Martin, 'Dalmeny House, West Lothian', *Country Life*, August 17 and 24, 1989

ROSEBERY, Countess of, *Dalmeny House*, Dalmeny

RYKWERT, Joseph, and RYKWERT,

Anne, *The Brothers Adam*, London, 1985

SAYER, Michael, and MASSINGBERD, Hugh, *The Disintegration of a Heritage: Country Houses and their Collections*, Wilby, 1993

SAVAGE, Peter, *Lorimer and the Edinburgh Craft Designers*, Edinburgh, 1980

SITWELL, Sacheverell, *British Architects and Craftsmen*, London, 1945

SMALL, *Castles and Mansions of the Lothians*, Edinburgh, 1883

SMOUT, T.C., *History of the Scottish People 1560–1830*, London, 1969

STAMP, Gavin (ed), *Mount Stuart House and Gardens*, Mount Stuart, 1995

STEWART, A.F. (ed), *Horace Walpole: Last Journals*, London, 1910

STEWART, J.L.M., *The Story of the Atholl Highlanders*, Blair Atholl, 1987

STIRLING MAXWELL, Sir John, Bt, *Scottish Homes and Shrines*, London, 1938

STORMONTH DARLING, Sir Jamie, and PRENTICE, Robin, *Culzean: The Continuing Challenge*, Edinburgh,1985

STRONG, Roy, BINNEY, Marcus, HARRIS, John *et al*, *The Destruction of the Country House*, London, 1974

STUART, Denis, *Dear Duchess: Millicent Duchess of Sutherland 1867–1955*, London, 1982

SUTHERLAND, Douglas, *The Landowners*, London, 1968

SYKES, Christopher Simon, *Black Sheep*, London, 1982

TAIT, A.A., *Duff House*, Edinburgh, 1985

— *Treasures in Trust*, Edinburgh, 1981

TAIT, J.G. (ed), *Sir Walter Scott's Journal*, Edinburgh, 1939–46 (3 vols)

WALKER, N.H., *Kinross House*, 1990

INDEX